THE MODERN DRAMA SERIES
EDITED BY EDWIN BJÖRKMAN

THE GODS OF THE MOUNTAIN : THE GOLDEN
DOOM : KING ARGIMĒNĒS AND THE UN-
KNOWN WARRIOR: THE GLITTERING GATE:
THE LOST SILK HAT : BY LORD DUNSANY

FIVE PLAYS

THE GODS OF THE MOUNTAIN
THE GOLDEN DOOM
KING ARGIMĒNĒS AND THE UNKNOWN WARRIOR
THE GLITTERING GATE
THE LOST SILK HAT

BY

LORD DUNSANY

BOSTON
LITTLE, BROWN, AND COMPANY
1918

COMPOSITION AND ELECTROTYPING BY
THE PLIMPTON PRESS · NORWOOD · MASS · U · S · A
PRESSWORK BY S. J. PARKHILL & CO. BOSTON

CONTENTS

INTRODUCTION

Reason

OBSERVATION and imagination are the basic principles of all poetry. It is impossible to conceive a poetical work from which one of them is wholly absent. Observation without imagination makes for obviousness; imagination without observation turns into nonsense. What marks the world's greatest poetry is perhaps the presence in almost equal proportion of both these principles. But as a rule we find one of them predominating, and from this one-sided emphasis the poetry of the period derives its character as realistic or idealistic.

The poetry of the middle nineteenth century made a fetish of observation. It came as near excluding imagination as it could without ceasing entirely to be poetry. That such exaggeration should sooner or later result in a sharp reaction was natural. The change began during the eighties and gathered full headway in the early nineties. Imagination, so long scorned, came into its rights once more, and it is rapidly becoming the dominant note in the literary production of our own day.

The new movement has been called " neo-romantic " and " symbolistic." Both these names apply, but neither of them exhausts the contents or meaning of the movement which received its first impetus from Ibsen and which later found its typical embodiment in Maeterlinck. From this movement came much of

the inspiration that produced the poetical re-birth of
Ireland out of which has sprung the man whom I have
now the pleasure of introducing to American readers:
a man with imagination as elfish as moonlight mist.

Edward John Moreton Drax Plunkett, Lord Dunsany, is the eighteenth member of his family to bear
the title which gives him a place in the Irish peerage.
He was born in 1878 and received his education at
Eton and Sandhurst. In 1899 he succeeded his father
to the title and the family estate in Meath, Ireland.
During the South African war he served at the front
with the Coldstream Guards. He is passionately fond
of outdoor life and often spends the whole day in the
saddle before sitting down at his desk to write late
at night.

His work proves, however, that he is as fond of
spiritual as of physical exercise, and that he is an
inveterate traveller in those mysterious regions of the
partly known or wholly unknown where the imagination alone can guide us. His first literary heroes were
the brothers Grimm and Andersen. Then the Greek
world of Olympians was revealed to him, making a
lasting impression on his mind. But it was the Bible
that gave him the limpid style which makes his most
fantastic tales as real as government reports — or
rather much more so. "For years no style seemed to
me natural but that of the Bible," he said not long
ago, "and I feared that I would never become a writer
when I saw that other people did not use it."

For something like ten years he has been a pretty
frequent and increasingly valued contributor to English and Anglo-Irish periodicals. He has previously
published five volumes: "The Gods of Pegana," 1905;

"Time and the Gods," 1906; "The Sword of Welleran," 1908; "A Dreamer's Tales," 1910; and "The Book of Wonder," 1912. All are collections of prose pieces that defy accepted classifications. They are fairy tales and short stories and essays and prose poems at the same time.

The reader has only to take a brief glance at one of those works to make the astounding discovery that he is being introduced to worlds of which he has never heard before. Even the "Arabian Nights" have a clearly identifiable background of popular legend and myth. Nothing of the kind is to be found in the writings of Lord Dunsany. He may be said to have created a new mythology wholly his own. He is not only the master but the maker of the countries to which he takes us on such fascinating jaunts. His commonest name for them is the Edge of the World, but sometimes he speaks of them as the Lands of Wonder. This latter name is doubly significant, for the whole movement of which he forms such a striking manifestation has been defined as a "renascence of wonder."

The names of places and persons appearing in the stories of Lord Dunsany are worth a study in themselves. There are hundreds of them, giving evidence of an inexhaustible imagination; and each one of them is as aptly suggestive as if generations of men had been at work shaping them. To hear of Sardathion, the city built by the Gods of Old, is to see its domes of marble rising sky-high in the sunset-lighted air. To hear of Slith and Sippy and Slorg, the three thieves who went to the Edge of the World in quest of the Golden Box, is to feel as if one were dealing with historical characters like Aaron Burr or Chinese Gordon. And as we learn more about them, these fanciful creatures of Lord Dunsany's brain assume still more familiar characteristics, as if they had been studied in some Irish village or English street. It is this fact that reveals one of the main secrets of Lord Dunsany's appeal: that behind all his exuberant imagination lies a solid basis of observation, enabling him to endow the most impossible adventures with a homely and convincing air.

The five plays contained in the present volume have all been produced on the stage. "The Golden Doom" and "The Gods of the Mountain" have been staged most successfully at the Haymarket Theatre, London. "King Argimēnēs" and "The Glittering Gate" have been given by the Irish Players, and "The Lost Silk Hat" has been put on by Iden Payne at Manchester. In America, the first three have been in the repertoire of Stuart Walker's Portmanteau Theatre, and "The Glittering Gate" has been given by the Neighborhood Players.

After seeing "The Gods of the Mountain," Frank Harris wrote: "It was one of the nights of my life; the only play, I said to myself, which meant anything to me in twenty years or more." Without sharing the opinion of Mr. Harris about the dramatic output of the last twenty years, I share fully his enthusiasm in regard to the play that caused his remark. The note struck in it is so distinctly new as to make one gasp as under a sharp shock. But the surprise turns quickly into pleasure such as only the originality of genius can confer.

It is hard to define just what makes these plays what they are. But certain qualities are tangible.

Their deep and rich symbolism is one. It is the kind of symbolism for which the advances of modern psychology had prepared us — the kind that is inseparable from life itself as we are only just beginning to understand it. Another quality is their capacity for suggesting at once the intimate unity and appalling vastness of life. In "The Golden Doom" the fate of an empire and a little boy's desire for a new plaything become linked as facts of equal importance in the web of fate. In "The Gods of the Mountain" we meet with an atmosphere of fatality comparable only to that found in the Greek dramas. The crime of *hybris*, which to the Greeks was the "unforgivable sin," is here made as real to us as it was to them.

But these remarks of mine about the inner significance of the plays should not tempt anybody into thinking them deficient in that element of formal perfection without which they could not be classed as works of art. They are, indeed, "things of beauty," and their beauty inheres in their design as well as in their style. Through all of them the greatest possible economy of means has been observed, so that not a word, not a tone, not a gesture is wasted in obtaining the effect aimed at. The dialogue of Maeterlinck is suggested, but not more than suggested. The words spoken by the characters of Maeterlinck are often so vague as to be practically meaningless. The characters of Lord Dunsany speak as simply as those of Maeterlinck, but always sharply to the point; there can be no mistaking of what they mean, and that meaning serves always to carry the action of the play forward. And each play of Lord Dunsany's is an exciting adventure, conveying to the reader an exhilarating sense of motion without ever descending to old-fashioned stage tricks for the production of that sense. This means that they combine to an extraordinary degree the qualities which make separately for theatrical or literary success.

EDWIN BJÖRKMAN.

CHRONOLOGICAL LIST OF PLAYS
BY LORD DUNSANY

THE GODS OF THE MOUNTAIN

PERSONS

AGMAR
SLAG
ULF
OOGNO } *Beggars*
THAHN
MLAN
A THIEF

OORANDER
ILLANAUN } *Citizens*
AKMOS

THE DROMEDARY MEN
CITIZENS, ETC.
THE OTHERS

SCENE: THE EAST

THE GODS OF THE MOUNTAIN

THE FIRST ACT

Outside a city wall. Three beggars are seated upon the ground.

OOGNO

These days are bad for beggary.

THAHN

They are bad.

ULF (*an older beggar but not gray*)

Some evil has befallen the rich ones of this city. They take no joy any longer in benevolence, but are become sour and miserly at heart. Alas for them! I sometimes sigh for them when I think of this.

OOGNO

Alas for them! A miserly heart must be a sore affliction.

THAHN

A sore affliction indeed, and bad for our calling.

OOGNO (*reflectively*)

They have been thus for many months. What thing has befallen them?

THAHN

Some evil thing.

ULF

There has been a comet come near to the earth of

late and the earth has been parched and sultry so that the gods are drowsy and all those things that are divine in man, such as benevolence, drunkenness, extravagance, and song, have faded and died and have not been replenished by the gods.

OOGNO

It has indeed been sultry.

THAHN

I have seen the comet o' nights.

ULF

The gods are drowsy.

OOGNO

If they awake not soon and make this city worthy again of our order I for one shall forsake the calling and buy a shop and sit at ease in the shade and barter for gain.

THAHN

You will keep a shop?

[*Enter Agmar and Slag. Agmar, though poorly dressed, is tall, imperious, and older than Ulf. Slag follows behind him.*

AGMAR

Is this a beggar who speaks?

OOGNO

Yes, master, a poor beggar.

AGMAR

How long has the calling of beggary existed?

OOGNO

Since the building of the first city, master.

AGMAR

And when has a beggar ever followed a trade? When has he ever haggled and bartered and sat in a shop?

OOGNO

Why, he has never done so.

AGMAR

Are you he that shall be first to forsake the calling?

OOGNO

Times are bad for the calling here.

THAHN

They are bad.

AGMAR

So you would forsake the calling?

OOGNO

The city is unworthy of our calling. The gods are drowsy and all that is divine in man is dead. (*To third beggar*) Are not the gods drowsy?

ULF

They are drowsy in their mountains away at Marma. The seven green idols are drowsy. Who is this that rebukes us?

THAHN

Are you some great merchant, master? Perhaps you will help a poor man that is starving.

SLAG

My master a merchant! No, no. He is no merchant. My master is no merchant.

OOGNO

I perceive that he is some lord in disguise. The gods have woken and have sent him to save us.

SLAG

No, no. You do not know my master. You do not know him.

THAHN

Is he the Soldan's self that has come to rebuke us?

AGMAR

I am a beggar, and an old beggar.

SLAG (*with great pride*)

There is none like my master. No traveller has met with cunning like to his, not even those that come from Æthiopia.

ULF

We make you welcome to our town, upon which an evil has fallen, the days being bad for beggary.

AGMAR

Let none who has known the mystery of roads or has felt the wind arising new in the morning, or who has called forth out of the souls of men divine benevolence, ever speak any more of any trade or of the miserable gains of shops and the trading men.

OOGNO

I but spoke hastily, the times being bad.

AGMAR

I will put right the times.

SLAG

There is nothing that my master cannot do.

AGMAR (*to Slag*)

Be silent and attend to me. I do not know this city. I have travelled from far, having somewhat exhausted the city of Ackara.

SLAG

My master was three times knocked down and injured by carriages there, once he was killed and seven times beaten and robbed, and every time he was generously compensated. He had nine diseases, many of them mortal —

AGMAR

Be silent, Slag. — Have you any thieves among the calling here?

ULF

We have a few that we call thieves here, master, but they would scarcely seem thieves to you. They are not good thieves.

AGMAR

I shall need the best thief you have.
[*Enter two citizens richly clad, Illanaun and Oo-rander.*

ILLANAUN

Therefore we will send galleons to Ardaspes.

OORANDER

Right to Ardaspes through the silver gates.
[*Agmar transfers the thick handle of his long staff to his left armpit, he droops on to it and it supports his weight; he is upright no longer. His right arm hangs limp and useless. He hobbles up to the citizens imploring alms.*

ILLANAUN

I am sorry. I cannot help you. There have been too many beggars here and we must decline alms for the good of the town.

AGMAR (*sitting down and weeping*)

I have come from far.
[*Illanaun presently returns and gives Agmar a coin. Exit Illanaun. Agmar, erect again, walks back to the others.*

AGMAR

We shall need fine raiment; let the thief start at once. Let it rather be green raiment.

BEGGAR

I will go and fetch the thief. (*Exit*)

ULF

We will dress ourselves as lords and impose upon the city.

OOGNO

Yes, yes; we will say we are ambassadors from a far land.

ULF

And there will be good eating.

SLAG (*in an undertone to Ulf*)

But you do not know my master. Now that you have suggested that we shall go as lords, he will make a better suggestion. He will suggest that we should go as kings.

ULF

Beggars as kings!

SLAG

Ay. You do not know my master.

ULF (*to Agmar*)

What do you bid us do?

AGMAR

You shall first come by the fine raiment in the manner I have mentioned.

ULF

And what then, master?

AGMAR

Why, then we shall go as gods.

BEGGARS

As gods!

AGMAR

As gods. Know you the land through which I have lately come in my wanderings? Marma, where the gods are carved from green stone in the mountains. They sit all seven of them against the hills. They sit there motionless and travellers worship them.

ULF

Yes, yes, we know those gods. They are much reverenced here, but they are drowsy and send us nothing beautiful.

AGMAR

They are of green jade. They sit cross-legged with their right elbows resting on their left hands, the right forefinger pointing upward. We will come into the city disguised, from the direction of Marma, and will claim to be these gods. We must be seven as they are. And when we sit we must sit cross-legged as they do, with the right hand uplifted.

ULF

This is a bad city in which to fall into the hands of oppressors, for the judges lack amiability here as the merchants lack benevolence, ever since the gods forgot them.

AGMAR

In our ancient calling a man may sit at one street corner for fifty years doing the one thing, and yet a day may come when it is well for him to rise up and do another thing while the timorous man starves.

ULF

Also it were well not to anger the gods.

AGMAR

Is not all life a beggary to the gods? Do they not see all men always begging of them and asking alms with incense, and bells, and subtle devices?

OOGNO

Yes, all men indeed are beggars before the gods.

AGMAR

Does not the mighty Soldan often sit by the agate altar in his royal temple as we sit at a street corner or by a palace gate?

ULF

It is even so.

AGMAR

Then will the gods be glad when we follow the holy calling with new devices and with subtlety, as they are glad when the priests sing a new song.

ULF

Yet I have a fear.

[*Enter two men talking.*

AGMAR (*to Slag*)

Go you into the city before us and let there be a prophecy there which saith that the gods who are carven from green rock in the mountain shall one day arise in Marma and come here in the guise of men.

SLAG

Yes, master. Shall I make the prophecy myself? Or shall it be found in some old document?

AGMAR

Let someone have seen it once in some rare document. Let it be spoken of in the market place.

SLAG

It shall be spoken of, master.

[*Slag lingers. Enter Thief and Thahn.*

OOGNO

This is our thief.

AGMAR (*encouragingly*)

Ah, he is a quick thief.

THIEF

I could only procure you three green raiments, master. The city is not now well supplied with them; moreover, it is a very suspicious city and without shame for the baseness of its suspicions.

SLAG (*to a beggar*)

This is not thieving.

THIEF

I could do no more, master. I have not practised thieving all my life.

AGMAR

You have got something: it may serve our purpose. How long have you been thieving?

THIEF

I stole first when I was ten.

SLAG (*in horror*)

When he was ten!

AGMAR

We must tear them up and divide them amongst the seven. (*To Thahn*) Bring me another beggar.

SLAG

When my master was ten he had already to slip by night out of two cities.

OOGNO (*admiringly*)

Out of two cities?

SLAG (*nodding his head*)

In his native city they do not now know what became of the golden cup that stood in the Lunar Temple.

AGMAR

Yes, into seven pieces.

ULF

We will each wear a piece of it over our rags.

OOGNO

Yes, yes, we shall look fine.

AGMAR

That is not the way that we shall disguise ourselves.

OOGNO

Not cover our rags?

AGMAR

No, no. The first who looked closely would say, "These are only beggars. They have disguised themselves."

ULF

What shall we do?

AGMAR

Each of the seven shall wear a piece of the green raiment underneath his rags. And peradventure here and there a little shall show through; and men shall say, "These seven have disguised themselves as beggars. But we know not what they be."

SLAG

Hear my wise master.

OOGNO (*in admiration*)

He is a beggar.

ULF

He is an *old* beggar.

CURTAIN

THE SECOND ACT

The Metropolitan Hall of the city of Kongros.
Citizens, etc.

Enter the seven beggars with green silk under their
rags.

OORANDER
Who are you and whence come you?

AGMAR
Who may say what we are or whence we come?

OORANDER
What are these beggars and why do they come here?

AGMAR
Who said to you that we were beggars?

OORANDER
Why do these men come here?

AGMAR
Who said to you that we were men?

ILLANAUN
Now, by the moon!

AGMAR
My sister.

ILLANAUN
What?

AGMAR
My little sister.

SLAG
Our little sister the moon. She comes to us at
evenings away in the mountains of Marma. She

trips over the mountains when she is young. When she is young and slender she comes and dances before us, and when she is old and unshapely she hobbles away from the hills.

AGMAR

Yet is she young again and forever nimble with youth; yet she comes dancing back. The years are not able to curb her nor to bring gray hairs to her brethren.

OORANDER

This is not wonted.

ILLANAUN

It is not in accordance with custom.

AKMOS

Prophecy hath not thought it.

SLAG

She comes to us new and nimble, remembering olden loves.

OORANDER

It were well that prophets should come and speak to us.

ILLANAUN

This hath not been in the past. Let prophets come. Let prophets speak to us of future things.
[*The beggars seat themselves upon the floor in the attitude of the seven gods of Marma.*

CITIZEN

I heard men speak to-day in the market place. They speak of a prophecy read somewhere of old. It says the seven gods shall come from Marma in the guise of men.

ILLANAUN

Is this a true prophecy?

OORANDER

It is all the prophecy we have. Man without prophecy is like a sailor going by night over uncharted seas. He knows not where are the rocks nor where the havens. To the man on watch all things ahead are black and the stars guide him not, for he knows not what they are.

ILLANAUN

Should we not investigate this prophecy?

OORANDER

Let us accept it. It is as the small, uncertain light of a lantern, carried it may be by a drunkard, but along the shore of some haven. Let us be guided.

AKMOS

It may be that they are but benevolent gods.

AGMAR

There is no benevolence greater than our benevolence.

ILLANAUN

Then we need do little: they portend no danger to us.

AGMAR

There is no anger greater than our anger.

OORANDER

Let us make sacrifice to them if they be gods.

AKMOS

We humbly worship you, if ye be gods.

ILLANAUN (*kneeling too*)

You are mightier than all men and hold high rank among other gods and are lords of this our city, and have the thunder as your plaything and the whirlwind and the eclipse and all the destinies of human tribes — if ye be gods.

AGMAR

Let the pestilence not fall at once upon this city, as it had indeed designed to; let not the earthquake swallow it all immediately up amid the howls of the thunder; let not infuriated armies overwhelm those that escape — if we be gods —

POPULACE (*in horror*)

If we be gods!

OORANDER

Come, let us sacrifice.

ILLANAUN

Bring lambs.

AKMOS

Quick! Quick! (*Exeunt some*)

SLAG (*with solemn air*)

This god is a very divine god.

THAHN

He is no common god.

MLAN

Indeed he has made us.

CITIZEN (*to Slag*)

He will not punish us, master? None of the gods will punish us? We will make a sacrifice, a good sacrifice.

ANOTHER

We will sacrifice a lamb that the priests have blessed.

FIRST CITIZEN

Master, you are not wroth with us?

SLAG

Who may say what cloudy dooms are rolling up in the mind of the eldest of the gods? He is no common god like us. Once a shepherd went by him in the mountains and doubted as he went. He sent a doom after that shepherd.

CITIZEN

Master, we have not doubted.

SLAG

And the doom found him on the hills at evening.

SECOND CITIZEN

It shall be a good sacrifice, master.

[*Reënter with a dead lamb and fruits. They offer the lamb on an altar where there is fire, and fruits before the altar.*

THAHN (*stretching out a hand to a lamb upon an altar*)   That leg is not being cooked at all.

ILLANAUN

It is strange that gods should be thus anxious about the cooking of a leg of lamb.

OORANDER

It is strange certainly.

ILLANAUN

Almost I had said that it was a man spoke then.

OORANDER (*stroking his beard and regarding the second beggar*)   Strange. Strange, certainly.

AGMAR

Is it then strange that the gods love roasted flesh? For this purpose they keep the lightning. When the lightning flickers about the limbs of men there comes to the gods in Marma a pleasant smell, even a smell of roasting. Sometimes the gods, being pacific, are pleased to have roasted instead the flesh of lamb. It is all one to the gods; let the roasting stop.

OORANDER

No, no, gods of the mountains!

OTHERS

　No, no.

OORANDER

　Quick, let us offer the flesh to them.　If they eat, all is well.

　[*They offer it;　the beggars eat, all but Agmar, who watches.*

ILLANAUN

　One who was ignorant, one who did not know, had almost said that they ate like hungry men.

OTHERS

　Hush!

AKMOS

　Yet they look as though they had not had a meal like this for a long time.

OORANDER

　They have a hungry look.

AGMAR (*who has not eaten*)

　I have not eaten since the world was very new and the flesh of men was tenderer than now.　These younger gods have learned the habit of eating from the lions.

OORANDER

　O oldest of divinities, partake, partake.

AGMAR

　It is not fitting that such as I should eat.　None eat but beasts and men and the younger gods.　The sun and the moon and the nimble lightning and I — we may kill and we may madden, but we do not eat.

AKMOS

　If he but eat of our offering he cannot overwhelm us.

ALL

Oh, ancient deity, partake, partake.

AGMAR

Enough. Let it be enough that these have condescended to this bestial and human habit.

ILLANAUN (*to Akmos*)

And yet he is not unlike a beggar whom I saw not so long since.

OORANDER

But beggars eat.

ILLANAUN

Now I never knew a beggar yet who would refuse a bowl of Woldery wine.

AKMOS

This is no beggar.

ILLANAUN

Nevertheless let us offer him a bowl of Woldery wine.

AKMOS

You do wrong to doubt him.

ILLANAUN

I do but wish to prove his divinity. I will fetch the Woldery wine. (*Exit*)

AKMOS

He will not drink. Yet if he does, then he will not overwhelm us. Let us offer him the wine.
[*Reënter Illanaun with a goblet.*

FIRST BEGGAR

It is Woldery wine!

SECOND BEGGAR

It is Woldery!

THIRD BEGGAR

A goblet of Woldery wine!

FOURTH BEGGAR

O blessed day!

MLAN

O happy times!

SLAG

O my wise master!

[*Illanaun takes the goblet. All the beggars stretch out their hands including Agmar. Illanaun gives it to Agmar. Agmar takes it solemnly, and very carefully pours it upon the ground.*

FIRST BEGGAR

He has spilt it.

SECOND BEGGAR

He has spilt it. (*Agmar sniffs the fumes, loquitur*)

AGMAR

It is a fitting libation. Our anger is somewhat appeased.

ANOTHER BEGGAR

But it was Woldery!

AKMOS (*kneeling to Agmar*)

Master, I am childless, and I —

AGMAR

Trouble us not now. It is the hour at which the gods are accustomed to speak to the gods in the language of the gods, and if Man heard us he would guess the futility of his destiny, which were not well for Man. Begone! Begone!

ONE LINGERS (*loquitur*)

Master —

AGMAR

Begone!

[*Exeunt. Agmar takes up a piece of meat and*

begins to eat it; the beggars rise and stretch them-
selves: they laugh, but Agmar eats hungrily.

OOGNO

Ah! Now we have come into our own.

THAHN

Now we have alms.

SLAG

Master! My wise master!

ULF

These are the good days, the good days; and yet
I have a fear.

SLAG

What do you fear? There is nothing to fear. No
man is as wise as my master.

ULF

I fear the gods whom we pretend to be.

SLAG

The gods?

AGMAR (*taking a chunk of meat from his lips*)
Come hither, Slag.

SLAG (*going up to him*)
Yes, master.

AGMAR

Watch in the doorway while I eat. (*Slag goes to
the doorway*) Sit in the attitude of a god. Warn
me if any of the citizens approach.

[*Slag sits in the doorway in the attitude of a god,
back to the audience.*

OOGNO (*to Agmar*)
But, master, shall we not have Woldery wine?

AGMAR

We shall have all things if only we are wise at first
for a little.

THAHN

Master, do any suspect us?

AGMAR

We must be *very* wise.

THAHN

But if we are not wise, master?

AGMAR

Why, then death may come to us —

THAHN

O master!

AGMAR

— slowly.

[*All stir uneasily except Slag, who sits motionless in the doorway.*

OOGNO

Do they believe us, master?

SLAG (*half turning his head*)

Someone comes.

[*Slag resumes his position.*

AGMAR (*putting away his meat*)

We shall soon know now.

[*All take up the attitude. Enter One, loquitur.*

ONE

Master, I want the god that does not eat.

AGMAR

I am he.

ONE

Master, my child was bitten in the throat by a death-adder at noon. Spare him, master; he still breathes, but slowly.

AGMAR

Is he indeed your child?

ONE

He is surely my child, master.

AGMAR

Was it your wont to thwart him in his play, while he was strong and well?

ONE

I never thwarted him, master.

AGMAR

Whose child is Death?

ONE

Death is the child of the gods.

AGMAR

Do you that never thwarted your child in his play ask this of the gods?

ONE (*with some horror, perceiving Agmar's meaning*) Master!

AGMAR

Weep not. For all the houses that men have builded are the play-fields of this child of the gods.

[*The Man goes away in silence, not weeping.*

OOGNO (*taking Thahn by the wrist*)

Is this indeed a man?

AGMAR

A man, a man, and until just now a hungry one.

CURTAIN

THE THIRD ACT

Same room.
A few days have elapsed.
Seven thrones shaped like mountain-crags stand along the back of the stage. On these the beggars are lounging. The Thief is absent.

MLAN

Never had beggars such a time.

OOGNO

Ah, the fruits and tender lamb!

THAHN

The Woldery wine!

SLAG

It was better to see my master's wise devices than to have fruit and lamb and Woldery wine.

MLAN

Ah! When they spied on him to see if he would eat when they went away!

OOGNO

When they questioned him concerning the gods and Man!

THAHN

When they asked him why the gods permitted cancer!

SLAG

Ah, my wise master!

MLAN

How well his scheme has succeeded!

OOGNO

How far away is hunger!

THAHN

It is even like to one of last year's dreams, the trouble of a brief night long ago.

OOGNO (*laughing*)

Ho, ho, ho! To see them pray to us.

AGMAR

When we were beggars did we not speak as beggars? Did we not whine as they? Was not our mien beggarly?

OOGNO

We were the pride of our calling.

AGMAR

Then now that we are gods, let us be as gods, and not mock our worshippers.

ULF

I think that the gods *do* mock their worshippers.

AGMAR

The gods have never mocked us. We are above all pinnacles that we have ever gazed at in dreams.

ULF

I think that when man is high then most of all are the gods wont to mock him.

THIEF (*entering*)

Master! I have been with those that know all and see all. I have been with the thieves, master. They know me for one of the craft, but they do not know me as being one of us.

AGMAR

Well, well!

THIEF

There is danger, master, there is great danger.

AGMAR

You mean that they suspect that we are men.

THIEF

That they have long done, master. I mean that they will know it. Then we are lost.

AGMAR

Then they do not know it.

THIEF

They do not know it yet, but they will know it, and we are lost.

AGMAR

When will they know it?

THIEF

Three days ago they suspected us.

AGMAR

More than you think suspected us, but have any dared to say so?

THIEF

No, master.

AGMAR

Then forget your fears, my thief.

THIEF

Two men went on dromedaries three days ago to see if the gods were still at Marma.

AGMAR

They went to Marma!

THIEF

Yes, three days ago.

OOGNO

We are lost!

AGMAR

They went three days ago?

THIEF

Yes, on dromedaries.

AGMAR

They should be back to-day.

OOGNO

We are lost!

THAHN

We are lost!

THIEF

They must have seen the green jade idols sitting against the mountains. They will say, " The gods are still at Marma." And we shall be burnt.

SLAG

My master will yet devise a plan.

AGMAR (*to the Thief*)

Slip away to some high place and look toward the desert and see how long we have to devise a plan.

SLAG

My master will find a plan.

OOGNO

He has taken us into a trap.

THAHN

His wisdom is our doom.

SLAG

He will find a wise plan yet.

THIEF (*reëntering*)

It is too late!

AGMAR

It is too late!

THIEF

The dromedary men are here.

OOGNO

We are lost!

AGMAR

Be silent! I must think.

[*They all sit still. Citizens enter and prostrate themselves. Agmar sits deep in thought.*

ILLANAUN (*to Agmar*)

Two holy pilgrims have gone to your sacred shrines, wherein you were wont to sit before you left the mountains. (*Agmar says nothing*) They return even now.

AGMAR

They left us here and went to find the gods? A fish once took a journey into a far country to find the sea.

ILLANAUN

Most reverend deity, their piety is so great that they have gone to worship even your shrines.

AGMAR

I know these men that have great piety. Such men have often prayed to me before, but their prayers are not acceptable. They little love the gods; their only care is their piety. I know these pious ones. They will say that the seven gods were still at Marma. They will lie and say that we were still at Marma. So shall they seem more pious to you all, pretending that they alone have seen the gods. Fools shall believe them and share in their damnation.

OORANDER (*to Illanaun*)

Hush! You anger the gods.

ILLANAUN

I am not sure whom I anger.

OORANDER

It may be they are the gods.

ILLANAUN

Where are these men from Marma?

CITIZEN

Here are the dromedary men; they are coming now.

ILLANAUN (*to Agmar*)

The holy pilgrims from your shrine are come to worship you.

AGMAR

The men are doubters. How the gods hate the word! Doubt ever contaminated virtue. Let them be cast into prison and not besmirch your purity. (*Rising*) Let them not enter here.

ILLANAUN

But oh, most reverend deity from the Mountain, we also doubt, most reverend deity.

AGMAR

You have chosen. You have chosen. And yet it is not too late. Repent and cast these men in prison and it may not be too late. *The gods have never wept.* And yet when they think upon damnation and the dooms that are withering a myriad bones, then almost, were they not divine, they could weep. Be quick! Repent of your doubt.

[*Enter the Dromedary Men.*

ILLANAUN

Most reverend deity, it is a mighty doubt.

CITIZENS

Nothing has killed him! They are not the gods!

SLAG (*to Agmar*)

You have a plan, my master. You have a plan.

AGMAR

Not yet, Slag.

ILLANAUN (*to Oorander*)

These are the men that went to the shrines at
Marma.

OORANDER (*in a loud, clear voice*)

Were the Gods of the Mountain seated still at
Marma, or were they not there?

[*The beggars get up hurriedly from their thrones.*

DROMEDARY MAN

They were not there.

ILLANAUN

They were not there?

DROMEDARY MAN

Their shrines were empty.

OORANDER

Behold the Gods of the Mountain!

AKMOS

They have indeed come from Marma.

OORANDER

Come. Let us go away to prepare a sacrifice. A
mighty sacrifice to atone for our doubting. (*Exeunt*)

SLAG

My most wise master!

AGMAR

No, no, Slag. I do not know what has befallen.
When I went by Marma only two weeks ago the
idols of green jade were still seated there.

OOGNO

We are saved now.

THAHN

Ay, we are saved.

AGMAR

We are saved, but I know not how.

OOGNO

Never had beggars such a time.

THIEF

I will go out and watch. (*He creeps out*)

ULF

Yet I have a fear.

OOGNO

A fear? Why, we are saved.

ULF

Last night I dreamed.

OOGNO

What was your dream?

ULF

It was nothing. I dreamed that I was thirsty and one gave me Woldery wine; yet there was a fear in my dream.

THAHN

When I drink Woldery wine I am afraid of nothing.

THIEF (*reëntering*)

They are making a pleasant banquet ready for us; they are killing lambs, and girls are there with fruits, and there is to be much Woldery wine.

MLAN

Never had beggars such a time.

AGMAR

Do any doubt us now?

THIEF

I do not know.

MLAN

When will the banquet be?

THIEF

When the stars come out.

OOGNO

Ah! It is sunset already. There will be good eating.

THAHN

We shall see the girls come in with baskets upon their heads.

OOGNO

There will be fruits in the baskets.

THAHN

All the fruits of the valley.

MLAN

Oh, how long we have wandered along the ways of the world!

SLAG

Oh, how hard they were!

THAHN

And how dusty!

OOGNO

And how little wine!

MLAN

How long we have asked and asked, and for how much!

AGMAR

We to whom all things are coming now at last!

THIEF

I fear lest my art forsake me now that good things come without stealing.

AGMAR

You will need your art no longer.

SLAG

The wisdom of my master shall suffice us all our days.

[*Enter a frightened Man. He kneels before Agmar
and abases his forehead.*

MAN

Master, we implore you, the people beseech you.
[*Agmar and the beggars in the attitude of the gods
sit silent.*

MAN

Master, it is terrible. (*The beggars maintain silence*) It is terrible when you wander in the evening. It is terrible on the edge of the desert in the
evening. Children die when they see you.

AGMAR

In the desert? When did you see us?

MAN

Last night, master. You were terrible last night.
You were terrible in the gloaming. When your
hands were stretched out and groping. You were
feeling for the city.

AGMAR

Last night do you say?

MAN

You were terrible in the gloaming!

AGMAR

You yourself saw us?

MAN

Yes, master, you were terrible. Children too saw
you and they died.

AGMAR

You say you saw us?

MAN

Yes, master. Not as you are now, but otherwise.
We implore you, master, not to wander at evening.
You are terrible in the gloaming. You are —

AGMAR

You say we appeared not as we are now. How did we appear to you?

MAN

Otherwise, master, otherwise.

AGMAR

But how did we appear to you?

MAN

You were all green, master, all green in the gloaming, all of rock again as you used to be in the mountains. Master, we can bear to see you in flesh like men, but when we see rock walking it is terrible, it is terrible.

AGMAR

That is how we appeared to you?

MAN

Yes, master. Rock should not walk. When children see it they do not understand. Rock should not walk in the evening.

AGMAR

There have been doubters of late. Are they satisfied?

MAN

Master, they are terrified. Spare us, master.

AGMAR

It is wrong to doubt. Go and be faithful.
[*Exit Man.*

SLAG

What have they seen, master?

AGMAR

They have seen their own fears dancing in the desert. They have seen something green after the light was gone, and some child has told them a tale that it was us. I do not know what they have seen. What should they have seen?

ULF

Something was coming this way from the desert, he said.

SLAG

What should come from the desert?

AGMAR

They are a foolish people.

ULF

That man's white face has seen some frightful thing.

SLAG

A frightful thing?

ULF

That man's face has been near to some frightful thing.

AGMAR

It is only we that have frightened them and their fears have made them foolish.

[*Enter an Attendant with a torch or lantern which he places in a receptacle. Exit.*

THAHN

Now we shall see the faces of the girls when they come to the banquet.

MLAN

Never had beggars such a time.

AGMAR

Hark! They are coming. I hear footsteps.

THAHN

The dancing girls! They are coming!

THIEF

There is no sound of flutes, they said they would come with music.

OOGNO

What heavy boots they have; they sound like feet of stone.

THAHN

I do not like to hear their heavy tread. Those that would dance to *us* must be light of foot.

AGMAR

I shall not smile at them if they are not airy.

MLAN

They are coming very slowly. They should come nimbly to us.

THAHN

They should dance as they come. But the footfall is like the footfall of heavy crabs.

ULF (*in a loud voice, almost chanting*)

I have a fear, an old fear and a boding. We have done ill in the sight of the seven gods. Beggars we were and beggars we should have remained. We have given up our calling and come in sight of our doom. I will no longer let my fear be silent; it shall run about and cry; it shall go from me crying, like a dog from out of a doomed city; for my fear has seen calamity and has known an evil thing.

SLAG (*hoarsely*)

Master!

AGMAR (*rising*)

Come, come!

[*They listen. No one speaks. The stony boots come on. Enter in single file through door in right of back, a procession of seven green men, even hands*

*and faces are green; they wear greenstone sandals;
they walk with knees extremely wide apart, as having sat cross-legged for centuries; their right arms
and right forefingers point upward, right elbows
resting on left hands; they stoop grotesquely.
Halfway to the footlights they left wheel. They
pass in front of the seven beggars, now in terrified
attitudes, and six of them sit down in the attitude
described, with their backs to the audience. The
leader stands, still stooping.*

OOGNO (*cries out just as they wheel left*)

The Gods of the Mountain!

AGMAR (*hoarsely*)

Be still! They are dazzled by the light. They may
not see us.

[*The leading Green Thing points his forefinger at
the lantern — the flame turns green. When the six
are seated the leader points one by one at each of
the seven beggars, shooting out his forefinger at
them. As he does this each beggar in his turn
gathers himself back on to his throne and crosses
his legs, his right arm goes stiffly upward with forefinger erect, and a staring look of horror comes into
his eyes. In this attitude the beggars sit motionless while a green light falls upon their faces. The
gods go out.*

*Presently enter the Citizens, some with victuals and
fruit. One touches a beggar's arm and then another's.*

CITIZEN

They are cold; they have turned to stone.

[*All abase themselves, foreheads to the floor.*

ONE

We have doubted them. We have doubted them.

They have turned to stone because we have doubted
them.

ANOTHER

They were the true gods.

ALL

They were the true gods.

CURTAIN

THE GOLDEN DOOM

PERSONS

THE KING
CHAMBERLAIN
CHIEF PROPHET
GIRL
BOY
SPIES
FIRST PROPHET
SECOND PROPHET
FIRST SENTRY
SECOND SENTRY
STRANGER
ATTENDANTS

Scene: Outside the King's great door in Zericon.
Time: Some while before the fall of Babylon.

THE GOLDEN DOOM

Two Sentries pace to and fro, then halt, one on each side of the great door.

FIRST SENTRY

The day is deadly sultry.

SECOND SENTRY

I would that I were swimming down the Gyshon, on the cool side, under the fruit trees.

FIRST SENTRY

It is like to thunder or the fall of a dynasty.

SECOND SENTRY

It will grow cool by night-fall. Where is the King?

FIRST SENTRY

He rows in his golden barge with ambassadors or whispers with captains concerning future wars. The stars spare him!

SECOND SENTRY

Why do you say " the stars spare him "?

FIRST SENTRY

Because if a doom from the stars fall suddenly on a king it swallows up his people and all things round about him, and his palace falls and the walls of his city and citadel, and the apes come in from the woods and the large beasts from the desert, so that you would not say that a king had been there at all.

SECOND SENTRY

But why should a doom from the stars fall on the King?

FIRST SENTRY

Because he seldom placates them.

SECOND SENTRY

Ah! I have heard that said of him.

FIRST SENTRY

Who are the stars that a man should scorn them? Should they that rule the thunder, the plague and the earthquake withhold these things save for much prayer? Always ambassadors are with the King, and his commanders, come in from distant lands, prefects of cities and makers of the laws, but never the priests of the stars.

SECOND SENTRY

Hark! Was that thunder?

FIRST SENTRY

Believe me, the stars are angry.

[*Enter a Stranger. He wanders toward the King's door, gazing about him.*

SENTRIES (*lifting their spears at him*)

Go back! Go back!

STRANGER

Why?

FIRST SENTRY

It is death to touch the King's door.

STRANGER

I am a stranger from Thessaly.

FIRST SENTRY

It is death even for a stranger.

STRANGER

Your door is strangely sacred.

FIRST SENTRY

    It is death to touch it.

    [*The Stranger wanders off.*

    [*Enter two children hand in hand.*

BOY (*to the Sentry*)

    I want to see the King to pray for a hoop.

    [*The Sentry smiles.*

BOY (*pushes the door; to girl*)

    I cannot open it. (*To the Sentry*) Will it do as well if I pray to the King's door?

SENTRY

    Yes, quite as well. (*Turns to talk to the other Sentry*) Is there anyone in sight?

SECOND SENTRY (*shading his eyes*)

    Nothing but a dog, and he far out on the plain.

FIRST SENTRY

    Then we can talk awhile and eat bash.

BOY

    King's door, I want a little hoop.

    [*The Sentries take a little bash between finger and thumb from pouches and put that wholly forgotten drug to their lips.*

GIRL (*pointing*)

    My father is a taller soldier than that.

BOY

    My father can write. He taught me.

GIRL

    Ho! Writing frightens nobody. My father is a soldier.

BOY

    I have a lump of gold. I found it in the stream that runs down to Gyshon.

GIRL

I have a poem. I found it in my own head.

BOY

Is it a long poem?

GIRL

No. But it would have been only there were no more
rhymes for sky.

BOY

What is your poem?

GIRL

> I saw a purple bird
>   Go up against the sky
> And it went up and up
>   And round about did fly.

BOY

I saw it die.

GIRL

That does n't scan.

BOY

Oh, that does n't matter.

GIRL

Do you like my poem?

BOY

Birds are n't purple.

GIRL

My bird was.

BOY

Oh!

GIRL

Oh, you don't like my poem!

BOY

Yes, I do.

GIRL

No, you don't; you think it horrid.

BOY

No. I don't.

GIRL

Yes, you do. Why did n't you say you liked it? It is the only poem I ever made.

BOY

I do like it. I do like it.

GIRL

You don't, you don't!

BOY

Don't be angry. I 'll write it on the door for you.

GIRL

You 'll write it?

BOY

Yes, I can write it. My father taught me. I 'll write it with my lump of gold. It makes a yellow mark on the iron door.

GIRL

Oh, do write it! I would like to see it written like real poetry.

[*The Boy begins to write. The Girl watches.*

FIRST SENTRY

You see, we 'll be fighting again soon.

SECOND SENTRY

Only a little war. We never have more than a little war with the hill-folk.

FIRST SENTRY

When a man goes to fight, the curtains of the gods wax thicker than ever before between his eyes and the future; he may go to a great or to a little war.

SECOND SENTRY

There can only be a little war with the hill-folk.

FIRST SENTRY

Yet sometimes the gods laugh.

SECOND SENTRY

At whom?

FIRST SENTRY

At kings.

SECOND SENTRY

Why have you grown uneasy about this war in the hills?

FIRST SENTRY

Because the King is powerful beyond any of his fathers, and has more fighting men, more horses, and wealth that could have ransomed his father and his grandfather and dowered their queens and daughters; and every year his miners bring him more from the opal-mines and from the turquoise-quarries. He has grown very mighty.

SECOND SENTRY

Then he will the more easily crush the hill-folk in a little war.

FIRST SENTRY

When kings grow very mighty the stars grow very jealous.

BOY

I 've written your poem.

GIRL

Oh, have you really?

BOY

Yes, I 'll read it to you. (*He reads*)

> I saw a purple bird
>
> Go up against the sky

> And it went up and up
> And round about did fly.
> I saw it die.

GIRL

It does n't scan.

BOY

That does n't matter.

[*Enter furtively a Spy, who crosses stage and goes out. The Sentries cease to talk.*

GIRL

That man frightens me.

BOY

He is only one of the King's spies.

GIRL

But I don't like the King's spies. They frighten me.

BOY

Come on, then, we 'll run away.

SENTRY (*noticing the children again*)

Go away, go away! The King is coming, he will eat you.

[*The Boy throws a stone at the Sentry and runs out. Enter another Spy, who crosses the stage. Enter third Spy, who notices the door. He examines it and utters an owl-like whistle. No. 2 comes back. They do not speak. Both whistle. No. 3 comes. All examine the door. Enter the King and his Chamberlain. The King wears a purple robe. The Sentries smartly transfer their spears to their left hands and return their right arms to their right sides. They then lower their spears until their points are within an inch of the ground, at the same time raising their right hands above their heads. They stand for some moments thus. Then they lower their right arms to their right sides, at the same time raising their spears. In the next motion they take their spears into their right hands and lower the butts to the floor, where they were before, the spears slanting forward a little. Both Sentries must move together precisely.*

FIRST SPY (*runs forward to the King and kneels, abasing his forehead to the floor*) Something has written on the iron door.

CHAMBERLAIN

On the iron door!

KING

Some fool has done it. Who has been here since yesterday?

FIRST SENTRY (*shifts his hand a little higher on his spear, brings the spear to his side and closes his heels all in one motion; he then takes one pace backward with his right foot; then he kneels on his right knee; when he has done this he speaks, but not before*) Nobody, Majesty, but a stranger from Thessaly.

KING

Did he touch the iron door?

FIRST SENTRY

No, Majesty; he tried to, but we drove him away.

KING

How near did he come?

FIRST SENTRY

Nearly to our spears, Majesty.

KING

What was his motive in seeking to touch the iron door?

FIRST SENTRY

I do not know, Majesty.

KING

Which way did he go?

FIRST SENTRY (*pointing left*)

That way, Majesty, an hour ago.

[*The King whispers with one of his Spies, who stoops and examines the ground and steals away. The Sentry rises.*

KING (*to his two remaining Spies*)

What does this writing say?

A SPY

We cannot read, Majesty.

KING

A good spy should know everything.

SECOND SPY

We watch, Majesty, and we search out, Majesty. We read shadows, and we read footprints, and whispers in secret places. But we do not read writing.

KING (*to the Chamberlain*)

See what it is.

CHAMBERLAIN (*goes up and reads*)

It is treason, Majesty.

KING

Read it.

CHAMBERLAIN

I saw a purple bird
　　Go up against the sky,
And it went up and up
　　And round about did fly.
　　　I saw it die.

FIRST SENTRY (*aside*)

The stars have spoken.

KING (*to the Sentry*)

Has anyone been here but the stranger from Thessaly?

SENTRY (*kneeling as before*)

Nobody, Majesty.

KING

You saw nothing?

FIRST SENTRY

Nothing but a dog far out upon the plain and the children of the guard at play.

KING (*to the Second Sentry*)

And you?

SECOND SENTRY (*kneeling*)

Nothing, Majesty.

CHAMBERLAIN

That is strange.

KING

It is some secret warning.

CHAMBERLAIN

It is treason.

KING

It is from the stars.

CHAMBERLAIN

No, no, Majesty. Not from the stars, not from the stars. Some man has done it. Yet the thing should be interpreted. Shall I send for the prophets of the stars?

[*The King beckons to his Spies. They run up to him.*

KING

Find me some prophet of the stars. (*Exeunt Spies*)

I fear that we may go no more, my chamberlain, along the winding ways of unequalled Zericon, nor play dahoori with the golden balls. I have thought more of my people than of the stars and more of Zericon than of windy Heaven.

CHAMBERLAIN

Believe me, Majesty, some idle man has written it and passed by. Your spies shall find him, and then his name will be soon forgotten.

KING

Yes, yes. Perhaps you are right, though the sentries saw no one. No doubt some beggar did it.

CHAMBERLAIN

Yes, Majesty, some beggar has surely done it. But look, here come two prophets of the stars. They shall tell us that this is idle.
[Enter two Prophets and a Boy attending them. All bow deeply to the King. The two Spies steal in again and stand at back.

KING

Some beggar has written a rhyme on the iron gate, and as the ways of rhyme are known to you I desired you, rather as poets than as prophets, to say whether there was any meaning in it.

CHAMBERLAIN

'T is but an idle rhyme.

FIRST PROPHET (bows again and goes up to door. He glances at the writing) Come hither, servant of those that serve the stars.
[Attendant approaches.

FIRST PROPHET

Bring hither our golden cloaks, for this may be a matter for rejoicing; and bring our green cloaks also, for this may tell of young new beautiful things

with which the stars will one day gladden the King;
and bring our black cloaks also, for it may be a
doom. (*Exit the Boy; the Prophet goes up to the
door and reads solemnly*) The stars have spoken.
[*Reënter Attendant with cloaks.*

KING

I tell you that some beggar has written this.

FIRST PROPHET

It is written in pure gold. (*He dons the black cloak
over body and head*)

KING

What do the stars mean? What warning is it?

FIRST PROPHET

I cannot say.

KING (*to Second Prophet*)

Come you then and tell us what the warning is.

SECOND PROPHET (*goes up to the door and reads*)

The stars have spoken. (*He cloaks himself in black*)

KING

What is it? What does it mean?

SECOND PROPHET

We do not know, but it is from the stars.

CHAMBERLAIN

It is a harmless thing; there is no harm in it, Majesty. Why should not birds die?

KING

Why have the prophets covered themselves in black?

CHAMBERLAIN

They are a secret people and look for inner mean-
ings. There is no harm in it.

KING

They have covered themselves in black.

CHAMBERLAIN

They have not spoken of any evil thing. They have not spoken of it.

KING

If the people see the prophets covered in black they will say that the stars are against me and believe that my luck has turned.

CHAMBERLAIN

The people must not know.

KING

Some prophet must interpret to us the doom. Let the chief prophet of the stars be sent for.

CHAMBERLAIN (*going toward left exit*)

Summon the chief prophet of the stars that look on Zericon.

VOICES OFF

The chief prophet of the stars. The chief prophet of the stars.

CHAMBERLAIN

I have summoned the chief prophet, Majesty.

KING

If he interpret this aright I will put a necklace of turquoises round his neck with opals from the mines.

CHAMBERLAIN

He will not fail. He is a very cunning interpreter.

KING

What if he covers himself with a huge black cloak and does not speak and goes muttering away, slowly with bended head, till our fear spreads to the sentries and they cry aloud?

CHAMBERLAIN

This is no doom from the stars, but some idle scribe

hath written it in his insolence upon the iron door, wasting his hoard of gold.

KING

Not for myself I have a fear of doom, not for myself; but I inherited a rocky land, windy and ill-nurtured, and nursed it to prosperity by years of peace and spread its boundaries by years of war. I have brought up harvests out of barren acres and given good laws unto naughty towns, and my people are happy, and lo, the stars are angry!

CHAMBERLAIN

It is not the stars, it is not the stars, Majesty, for the prophets of the stars have not interpreted it. Indeed, it was only some reveller wasting his gold.

[*Meanwhile enter Chief Prophet of the stars that look on Zericon.*

KING

Chief Prophet of the Stars that look on Zericon, I would have you interpret the rhyme upon yonder door.

CHIEF PROPHET (*goes up to the door and reads*)

It is from the stars.

KING

Interpret it and you shall have great turquoises round your neck, with opals from the mines in the frozen mountains.

CHIEF PROPHET (*cloaks himself like the others in a great black cloak*) Who should wear purple in the land but a King, or who go up against the sky but he who has troubled the stars by neglecting their ancient worship? Such a one has gone up and up increasing power and wealth, such a one has soared above the crowns of those that went before him,

such a one the stars have doomed, the undying ones,
the illustrious.   [*A pause.*

KING

Who wrote it?

CHIEF PROPHET

It is pure gold.   Some god has written it.

CHAMBERLAIN

Some god?

CHIEF PROPHET

Some god whose home is among the undying stars.

FIRST SENTRY (*aside to the Second Sentry*)

Last night I saw a star go flaming earthward.

KING

Is this a warning or is it a doom?

CHIEF PROPHET

The stars have spoken.

KING

It is, then, a doom?

CHIEF PROPHET

They speak not in jest.

KING

I have been a great King — Let it be said of me
" The stars overthrew him, and they sent a god for
his doom."   For I have not met my equal among
kings that man should overthrow me;   and I have
not oppressed my people that man should rise up
against me.

CHIEF PROPHET

It is better to give worship to the stars than to do
good to man.   It is better to be humble before the
gods than proud in the face of your enemy though
he do evil.

KING

Let the stars hearken yet and I will sacrifice a child to them — I will sacrifice a girl child to the twinkling stars and a male child to the stars that blink not, the stars of the steadfast eyes. (*To his Spies*) Let a boy and girl be brought for sacrifice. (*Exit a Spy to the right looking at footprints*) Will you accept this sacrifice to the god that the stars have sent? They say that the gods love children.

CHIEF PROPHET

I may refuse no sacrifice to the stars nor to the gods whom they send. (*To the other Prophets*) Make ready the sacrificial knives.

[*The Prophets draw knives and sharpen them.*

KING

Is it fitting that the sacrifice take place by the iron door where the god from the stars has trod, or must it be in the temple?

CHIEF PROPHET

Let it be offered by the iron door. (*To the other Prophets*) Fetch hither the altar stone.

[*The owl-like whistle is heard off right. The Third Spy runs crouching toward it. Exit.*

KING

Will this sacrifice avail to avert the doom?

CHIEF PROPHET

Who knows?

KING

I fear that even yet the doom will fall.

CHIEF PROPHET

It were wise to sacrifice some greater thing.

KING

What more can a man offer?

CHIEF PROPHET

His pride.

KING

What pride?

CHIEF PROPHET

Your pride that went up against the sky and troubled the stars.

KING

How shall I sacrifice my pride to the stars?

CHIEF PROPHET

It is upon your pride that the doom will fall, and will take away your crown and will take away your kingdom.

KING

I will sacrifice my crown and reign uncrowned amongst you, so only I save my kingdom.

CHIEF PROPHET

If you sacrifice your crown which is your pride, and if the stars accept it, perhaps the god that they sent may avert the doom and you may still reign in your kingdom though humbled and uncrowned.

KING

Shall I burn my crown with spices and with incense or cast it into the sea?

CHIEF PROPHET

Let it be laid here by the iron door where the god came who wrote the golden doom. When he comes again by night to shrivel up the city or to pour an enemy in through the iron door, he will see your cast-off pride and perhaps accept it and take it away to the neglected stars.

KING (*to the Chamberlain*)

Go after my spies and say that I make no sacrifice. (*Exit the Chamberlain to the right; the King takes off his crown*) Good-bye, my brittle glory; kings have sought you; the stars have envied you. (*The stage grows darker*)

CHIEF PROPHET

Even now the sun has set who denies the stars, and the day is departed wherein no gods walk abroad. It is near the hour when spirits roam the earth and all things that go unseen, and the faces of the abiding stars will be soon revealed to the fields. Lay your crown there and let us come away.

KING (*lays his crown before the iron door; then to the Sentries*) Go! And let no man come near the door all night.

THE SENTRIES (*kneeling*)

Yes, Majesty.

[*They remain kneeling until after the King has gone. King and the Chief Prophet walk away.*

CHIEF PROPHET

It was your pride. Let it be forgotten. May the stars accept it. (*Exeunt left*)

[*The Sentries rise.*

FIRST SENTRY

The stars have envied him!

SECOND SENTRY

It is an ancient crown. He wore it well.

FIRST SENTRY

May the stars accept it.

SECOND SENTRY

If they do not accept it what doom will overtake him?

FIRST SENTRY

It will suddenly be as though there were never any city of Zericon nor two sentries like you and me standing before the door.

SECOND SENTRY

Why! How do you know?

FIRST SENTRY

That is ever the way of the gods.

SECOND SENTRY

But it is unjust.

FIRST SENTRY

How should the gods know that?

SECOND SENTRY

Will it happen to-night?

FIRST SENTRY

Come! we must march away. (*Exeunt right*)

[*The stage grows increasingly darker. Reënter the Chamberlain from the right. He walks across the Stage and goes out to the left. Reënter Spies from the right. They cross the stage, which is now nearly dark.*

BOY (*enters from the right, dressed in white, his hands out a little, crying*) King's door, King's door, I want my little hoop. (*He goes up to the King's door. When he sees the King's crown there, he utters a satisfied*) O-oh! (*He takes it up, puts it on the ground, and, beating it before him with the sceptre, goes out by the way that he entered*)

[*The great door opens; there is light within; a furtive Spy slips out and sees that the crown is gone.*

Another Spy slips out. Their crouching heads come close together.

FIRST SPY (*hoarse whisper*)

The gods have come!

[*They run back through the door and the door is closed. It opens again and the King and the Chamberlain come through.*

KING

The stars are satisfied.

CURTAIN

KING ARGIMĒNĒS AND THE UNKNOWN WARRIOR

PERSONS

KING ARGIMĒNĒS
ZARB, *a slave born of slaves*
AN OLD SLAVE
A YOUNG SLAVE
SLAVES
} *Slaves of King Darniak*

KING DARNIAK
THE KING'S OVERSEER
A PROPHET
THE IDOL-GUARD
THE SERVANT OF THE KING'S DOG

QUEEN ATHARLIA
QUEEN OXARA
QUEEN CAHAFRA
QUEEN THRAGOLIND
} *Queens of King Darniak*

GUARDS AND ATTENDANTS

Time: A long time ago.

KING ARGIMĒNĒS AND THE UNKNOWN WARRIOR

THE FIRST ACT

The dinner-hour on the slave-fields of King Darniak. King Argimenes is sitting upon the ground, bowed, ragged and dirty, gnawing a bone. He has uncouth hair and a dishevelled beard. A battered spade lies near him. Two or three slaves sit at back of stage eating raw cabbage-leaves. The tear-song, the chant of the low-born, rises at intervals, monotonous and mournful, coming from distant slave-fields.

KING ARGIMENES

This is a good bone; there is juice in this bone.

ZARB

I wish I were you, Argimenes.

KING ARGIMENES

I am not to be envied any longer. I have eaten up my bone.

ZARB

I wish I were you, because you have been a king. Because men have prostrated themselves before your feet. Because you have ridden a horse and worn a crown and have been called Majesty.

KING ARGIMENES

When I remember that I have been a king it is very terrible.

ZARB

But you are lucky to have such things in your
memory as you have. I have nothing in my
memory — Once I went for a year without being
flogged, and I remember my cleverness in contriving
it — I have nothing else to remember.

KING ARGIMENES

It is very terrible to have been a king.

ZARB

But we have nothing who have no good memories
in the past. It is not easy for us to hope for the
future here.

KING ARGIMENES

Have you any god?

ZARB

We may not have a god because he might make us
brave and we might kill our guards. He might
make a miracle and give us swords.

KING ARGIMENES

Ah, you have no hope, then.

ZARB

I have a little hope. Hush, and I will tell you a
secret — The King's great dog is ill and like to
die. They will throw him to us. We shall have
beautiful bones then.

KING ARGIMENES

Ah! Bones.

ZARB

Yes. That is what *I* hope for. And have *you* no
other hope? Do you not hope that your nation
will arise some day and rescue you and cast off the
king and hang him up by his thumbs from the palace
gateway?

KING ARGIMENES

No. I have no other hope, for my god was cast down in the temple and broken into three pieces on the day that they surprised us and took me sleeping. But will they throw him to us? Will so honorable a brute as the King's dog be thrown to us?

ZARB

When he is dead his honors are taken away. Even the King when he is dead is given to the worms. Then why should not his dog be thrown to us?

KING ARGIMENES

We are not worms!

ZARB

You do not understand, Argimenes. The worms are little and free, while we are big and enslaved. I did not say we were worms, but we are *like* worms, and if they have the King when he is dead, why then —

KING ARGIMENES

Tell me more of the King's dog. Are there big bones on him?

ZARB

Ay, he is a big dog — a high, big, black one.

KING ARGIMENES

You know him then?

ZARB

Oh yes, I know him. I know him well. I was beaten once because of him, twenty-five strokes from the treble whips, two men beating me.

KING ARGIMENES

How did they beat you because of the King's dog?

ZARB

They beat me because I spoke to him without making obeisance. He was coming dancing along over the slave-fields and I spoke to him. He was a friendly great dog, and I spoke to him and patted his head, and did not make obeisance.

KING ARGIMENES

And they saw you do it?

ZARB

Yes, the slave-guard saw me. They came and seized me at once and bound my arms. The great dog wanted me to speak to him again, but I was hurried away.

KING ARGIMENES

You should have made obeisance.

ZARB

The great dog seemed so friendly that I forgot he was the King's great dog.

KING ARGIMENES

But tell me more. Was he hurt or is it a sickness?

ZARB

They say that it is a sickness.

KING ARGIMENES

Ah, then he will grow thin if he does not die soon. If it had been a hurt! — but we should not complain. I complain more often than you do because I had not learned to submit while I was yet young.

ZARB

If your beautiful memories do not please you, you should hope more. I wish I had your memories. I should not trouble to hope then. It is very hard to hope.

KING ARGIMENES

There will be nothing more to hope for when we have eaten the King's dog.

ZARB

Why, you might find gold in the earth while you were digging. Then you might bribe the commander of the guard to lend you his sword; we would all follow you if you had a sword. Then we might take the King and bind him and lay him on the ground and fasten his tongue outside his mouth with thorns and put honey on it and sprinkle honey near. Then the gray ants would come from one of their big mounds. My father found gold once when he was digging.

KING ARGIMENES (*pointedly*)

Did your father free himself?

ZARB

No. Because the King's Overseer found him looking at the gold and killed him. But he would have freed himself if he could have bribed the guard.

[*A Prophet walks across the stage attended by two guards.*

SLAVES

He is going to the King. He is going to the King.

ZARB

He is going to the King.

KING ARGIMENES

Going to prophesy good things to the King. It is easy to prophesy good things to a king, and be rewarded when the good things come. What else should come to a king? A prophet! A prophet!

[*A deep bell tolls slowly. King Argimenes and Zarb pick up their spades at once, and the old slaves at the back of the stage go down on their knees immediately and grub in the soil with their hands. The*

*white beard of the oldest trails in the dirt as he
works. King Argimenes digs.*

KING ARGIMENES

What is the name of that song that we always sing?
I like the song.

ZARB

It has no name. It is our song. There is no other
song.

KING ARGIMENES

Once there were other songs. Has this no name?

ZARB

I think the soldiers have a name for it.

KING ARGIMENES

What do the soldiers call it?

ZARB

The soldiers call it the tear-song, the chant of the
low-born.

KING ARGIMENES

It is a good song. I could sing no other now.

[*Zarb moves away digging.*

KING ARGIMENES (*to himself as his spade touches something in the earth*) Metal! (*Feels with his spade
again*) Gold perhaps!—It is of no use here.
(*Uncovers earth leisurely. Suddenly he drops on
his knees and works excitedly in the earth with his
hands. Then very slowly, still kneeling, he lifts,
lying flat on his hands, a long greenish sword, his
eyes intent on it. About the level of his uplifted
forehead he holds it, still flat on both hands, and
addresses it thus*) O holy and blessed thing! (*Then
he lowers it slowly till his hands rest on his knees,
and looking all the while at the sword, loquitur*)
Three years ago to-morrow King Darniak spat at

me, having taken my kingdom from me. Three
times in that year I was flogged, with twelve stripes,
with seventeen stripes, and with twenty stripes. A
year and eleven months ago, come Moon-day, the
King's Overseer struck me in the face, and nine
times in that year he called me dog. For one month
two weeks and a day I was yoked with a bullock
and pulled a rounded stone all day over the paths,
except while we were fed. I was flogged twice that
year — with eighteen stripes and with ten stripes.
This year the roof of the slave-sty has fallen in and
King Darniak will not repair it. Five weeks ago
one of his Queens laughed at me as she came across
the slave-fields. I was flogged again this year and
with thirteen stripes, and twelve times they have
called me dog. And these things they have done to
a king, and a king of the House of Ithara. (*He
listens attentively for a moment, then buries the
sword again and pats the earth over it with his
hands, then digs again*)

[*The old slaves do not see him: their faces are to
the earth. Enter the King's Overseer carrying a
whip. The slaves and King Argimenes kneel with
their foreheads to the ground as he passes across the
stage. Exit the King's Overseer.*]

KING ARGIMENES (*kneeling, hands outspread downward*)
O warrior spirit, wherever thou wanderest, whoever
be thy gods, whether they punish thee or whether
they bless thee, O kingly spirit, that once laid here
this sword, behold, I pray to thee, having no gods
to pray to, for the god of my nation was broken in
three by night. Mine arm is stiff with three years'
slavery, and remembers not the sword. But guide

thy sword till I have slain six men and armed the
strongest slaves, and thou shalt have the sacrifice
every year of a hundred goodly oxen.   And I will
build in Ithara a temple to thy memory wherein all
that enter in shall remember thee; so shalt thou be
honored and envied among the dead, for the dead
are very jealous of remembrance.   Ay, though thou
wert a robber that took men's lives unrighteously,
yet shall rare spices smoulder in thy temple and
little maidens sing and new-plucked flowers deck the
solemn aisles; and priests shall go about it ringing
bells that thy soul shall find repose.   Oh, but it has
a good blade, this old green sword; thou wouldst
not like to see it miss its mark (if the dead see at
all, as wise men teach), thou wouldst not like to see
it go thirsting into the air; so huge a sword should
find its marrowy bone.   (*Extending his right hand
upward*)   Come into my right arm, O ancient spirit,
O unknown warrior's soul!   And if thou hast the ear
of any gods, speak there against Illuriel, god of
King Darniak.   (*He rises and goes on digging*)

THE KING'S OVERSEER (*reëntering*)

So you have been praying.

KING ARGIMENES (*kneeling*)

No, master.

THE KING'S OVERSEER

The slave-guard saw you.   (*Strikes him*)   It is not
lawful for a slave to pray.

KING ARGIMENES

I did but pray to Illuriel to make me a good slave,
to teach me to dig well and to pull the rounded stone
and to make me not to die when the food is scarce,
but to be a good slave to my master the great King.

THE KING'S OVERSEER

Who art thou to pray to Illuriel? Dogs may not pray to an immortal god. (*Exit*)

[*Zarb comes back, digging.*

KING ARGIMENES (*digging*)

Zarb!

ZARB (*also digging*)

Do not look at me when you speak. The guards are watching us. Look at your digging.

KING ARGIMENES

How do the guards know we are speaking because we look at one another?

ZARB

You are very witless. Of course they know.

KING ARGIMENES

Zarb!

ZARB

What is it?

KING ARGIMENES

How many guards are there in sight?

ZARB

There are six of them over there. They are watching us.

KING ARGIMENES

Are there other guards in sight of these six guards?

ZARB

No.

KING ARGIMENES

How do you know?

ZARB

Because whenever their officer leaves them they sit upon the ground and play with dice.

KING ARGIMENES

How does that show that there are not another six in sight of them?

ZARB

How witless you are, Argimenes! Of course it shows there are not. Because, if there were, another officer would see them, and their thumbs would be cut off.

KING ARGIMENES

Ah! (*A pause*) Zarb! (*A pause*) Would the slaves follow me if I tried to kill the guards?

ZARB

No, Argimenes.

KING ARGIMENES

Why would they not follow me?

ZARB

Because you look like a slave. They will never follow a slave, because they are slaves themselves, and know how mean a creature is a slave. If you looked like a king they would follow you.

KING ARGIMENES

But I am a king. They know that I am a king.

ZARB

It is better to look like a king. It is looks that they would go by.

KING ARGIMENES

If I had a sword would they follow me? A beautiful huge sword of bronze.

ZARB

I wish I could think of things like that. It is because you were once a king that you can think of a sword of bronze. I tried to hope once that I should some day fight the guards, but I couldn't

picture a sword, I could n't imagine it; I could
only picture whips.

KING ARGIMENES

Dig a little nearer, Zarb. (*They both edge closer*)
I have found a very old sword in the earth. It is
not a sword such as common soldiers wear. A king
must have worn it, and an angry king. It must
have done fearful things; there are little dints in
it. Perhaps there was a battle here long ago where
all were slain, and perhaps that king died last and
buried his sword, but the great birds swallowed
him.

ZARB

You have been thinking too much of the King's dog,
Argimenes, and that has made you hungry, and
hunger has driven you mad.

KING ARGIMENES

I *have* found such a sword. [*A pause.*

ZARB

Why — then you will wear a purple cloak again,
and sit on a great throne, and ride a prancing horse,
and we shall call you Majesty.

KING ARGIMENES

I shall break a long fast first and drink much water,
and sleep. But will the slaves follow me?

ZARB

You will *make* them follow you if you have a sword.
Yet is Illuriel a very potent god. They say that
none have prevailed against King Darniak's dynasty
so long as Illuriel stood. Once an enemy cast Illuriel
into the river and overthrew the dynasty, but a
fisherman found him again and set him up, and the
enemy was driven out and the dynasty returned.

KING ARGIMENES

If Illuriel could be cast down as my god was cast
down perhaps King Darniak could be overcome as
I was overcome in my sleep?

ZARB

If Illuriel were cast down all the people would utter
a cry and flee away. It would be a fearful portent.

KING ARGIMENES

How many men are there in the armory at the
palace?

ZARB

There are ten men in the palace armory when all the
slave-guards are out.

[*They dig awhile in silence.*

ZARB

The officer of the slave-guard has gone away —
They are playing with dice now. (*He throws down
his spade and stretches his arms*) The man with
the big beard has won again, he is very nimble with
his thumbs — They are playing again, but it is
getting dark, I cannot clearly see.

[*King Argimenes furtively uncovers the sword, he
picks it up and grips it in his hand.*

ZARB

Majesty!

[*King Argimenes crouches and steals away towards
the slave-guard.*

.   .   .   .

ZARB (*to the other slaves*)

Argimenes has found a terrible sword and has gone
to slay the slave-guard. It is not a common sword,
it is some king's sword.

AN OLD SLAVE

Argimenes will be dreadfully flogged. We shall hear him cry all night. His cries will frighten us, and we shall not sleep.

ZARB

No, no! The guards flog poor slaves, but Argimenes had an angry look. The guards will be afraid when they see him look so angry and see his terrible sword. It was a huge sword, and he looked very angry. He will bring us the swords of the slave-guard. We must prostrate ourselves before him and kiss his feet or he will be angry with us too.

OLD SLAVE

Will Argimenes give me a sword?

ZARB

He will have swords for six of us if he slays the slave-guard. Yes, he will give you a sword.

SLAVE

A sword! No, no, I must not; the King would kill me if he found that I had a sword.

SECOND SLAVE (*slowly, as one who develops an idea*)

If the King found that I had a sword, why, then it would be an evil day for the King.

[*They all look off left.*

ZARB

I think that they are playing at dice again.

FIRST SLAVE

I do not see Argimenes.

ZARB

No, because he was crouching as he walked. The slave-guard is on the sky-line.

SECOND SLAVE

What is that dark shadow behind the slave-guard?

ZARB

It is too still to be Argimenes.

SECOND SLAVE

Look! It moves.

ZARB

The evening is too dark, I cannot see.

[*They continue to gaze into the gathering darkness. They raise themselves on their knees and crane their necks. Nobody speaks. Then from their lips and from others farther off goes up a long, deep " Oh! " It is like the sound that goes up from the grand-stand when a horse falls at a fence, or, in England, like the first exclamation of the crowd at a great cricket match when a man is caught in the slips.*

CURTAIN

THE SECOND ACT

The Throne Hall of King Darniak. The King is seated on his throne in the centre at the back of the stage; a little to his left, but standing out from the wall, a dark-green seated idol is set up. His Queens are seated about him on the ground, two on his right and two between him and the idol. All wear crowns. Beside the dark-green idol a soldier with a pike is kneeling upon one knee. The tear-song, the chant of the low-born, drifts faintly up from the slave-fields.

FIRST QUEEN

Do show us the new prophet, Majesty; it would be very interesting to see another prophet.

THE KING

Ah, yes.

[*He strikes upon a gong, and an Attendant enters, walks straight past the King and bows before the idol; he then walks back to the centre of the stage and bows before the King.*

THE KING

Bring the new prophet hither.

[*Exit Attendant. Enter the King's Overseer holding a roll of paper. He passes the King, bows to the idol, returns to the front of the King, kneels, and remains kneeling with bended head.*

THE KING (*speaking in the meanwhile to the Second Queen on his immediate right*) We are making a beautiful arbor for you, O Atharlia, at an end of the great garden. There shall be iris-flowers that you love and all things that grow by streams. And the stream there shall be small and winding like one of those in your country. I shall bring a stream a new way from the mountains. (*Turning to Queen Oxara on his extreme right*) And for you, too, O Oxara, we shall make a pleasance. I shall have rocks brought from the quarries for you, and my idle slaves shall make a hill and plant it with mountain shrubs, and you can sit there in the winter thinking of the North. (*To the kneeling Overseer*) Ah, what is here?

THE KING'S OVERSEER

The plans of your royal garden, Majesty. The slaves have dug it for five years and rolled the paths.

THE KING (*takes the plans*)

Was there not a garden in Babylon?

THE KING'S OVERSEER

They say there was a garden there of some sort, Majesty.

THE KING

I will have a greater garden. Let the world know and wonder. (*Looks at the plans*)

THE KING'S OVERSEER

It shall know at once, Majesty.

THE KING (*pointing at the plan*)

I do not like that hill, it is too steep.

THE KING'S OVERSEER

No, Majesty.

THE KING

Remove it.

THE KING'S OVERSEER

Yes, Majesty.

THE KING

When will the garden be ready for the Queens to walk in?

THE KING'S OVERSEER

Work is slow, Majesty, at this season of the year because the green stuff is scarce and the slaves grow idle. They even become insolent and ask for bones.

QUEEN CAHAFRA (*to the King's Overseer*)

Then *why* are they not flogged? (*To Queen Thragolind*) It is so simple, they *only* have to flog them, but these people are so silly sometimes. I want to walk in the great garden, and then they tell me: "It is not ready, Majesty. It is not ready, Majesty," as though there were any reason why it should *not* be ready.

FOURTH QUEEN

Yes, they are a great trouble to us.

[*Meanwhile the King hands back the plans. Exit the King's Overseer. Reënter Attendant with the Prophet, who is dressed in a long dark brown cloak; his face is solemn; he has a long dark beard and long hair. Having bowed before the idol, he bows before the King and stands silent. The attendant, having bowed to both, stands by the doorway.*

THE KING (*meanwhile to Queen Atharlia*)

Perhaps we shall lure the ducks when the marshes are frozen to come and swim in your stream; it will be like your own country. (*To the Prophet*) Prophesy unto us.

THE PROPHET (*speaks at once in a loud voice*)

There was once a King that had slaves to hate him

and to toil for him, and he had soldiers to guard him and to die for him. And the number of the slaves that he had to hate him and to toil for him was greater than the number of the soldiers that he had to guard him and to die for him. And the days of that King were few. And the number of thy slaves, O King, that thou hast to hate thee is greater than the number of thy soldiers.

QUEEN CAHAFRA (*to Queen Thragolind*)

— and I wore the crown with the sapphires and the big emerald in it, and the foreign prince said that I looked very sweet.

[*The King, who has been smiling at Atharlia, gives a gracious nod to the Prophet when he hears him stop speaking. When the Queens see the King nod graciously, they applaud the Prophet by idly clapping their hands.*

THIRD QUEEN

Do ask him to make us another prophecy, Majesty! He is so interesting. He looks so clever.

THE KING

Prophesy unto us.

THE PROPHET

Thine armies camped upon thy mountainous borders descry no enemy in the plains afar. And within thy gates lurks he for whom thy sentinels seek upon lonely guarded frontiers. There is a fear upon me and a boding. Even yet there is time, even yet; but *little* time. And my mind is dark with trouble for thy kingdom.

QUEEN CAHAFRA (*to Queen Thragolind*)

I do not like the way he does his hair.

QUEEN THRAGOLIND

· It would be all right if he would only have it cut.

THE KING (*to the Prophet, dismissing him with a nod of the head*)   Thank you, that has been very interesting.

QUEEN THRAGOLIND

How clever he is! I wonder how he thinks of things like that?

QUEEN CAHAFRA

Yes, but I hate a man who is conceited about it. Look how he wears his hair.

QUEEN THRAGOLIND

Yes, of course, it is perfectly dreadful.

QUEEN CAHAFRA

Why can't he wear his hair like other people, even if he does say clever things?

QUEEN THRAGOLIND

Yes, I hate a conceited man.[1]

[*Enter an Attendant. He bows before the idol, then kneels to the King.*

THE ATTENDANT

The guests are all assembled in the Chamber of Banquets.

[*All rise. The Queens walk two abreast to the Chamber of Banquets.*

QUEEN ATHARLIA (*to Queen Oxara*)

What was he talking about?

QUEEN OXARA

He was talking about the armies on the frontier.

---

[1] It is not necessary for the prophet's hair to be at all unusual.

QUEEN ATHARLIA

Ah! That reminds me of that young captain in the Purple Guard. They say that he loves Linoora.

QUEEN OXARA

Oh, Thearkos! Linoora probably said that.

[*When the Queens come to the doorway they halt on each side of it. Then they turn facing one another. Then the King leaves his throne and passes between them into the Chamber of Banquets, each couple courtseying low to him as he passes. The Queens follow, then the attendants. There rises the wine-song, the chant of the nobles, drowning the chant of the low-born. Only the Idol-Guard remains behind, still kneeling beside Illuriel.*

THE IDOL-GUARD

I do not like those things the Prophet said — It would be terrible if they were true — It would be very terrible if they were false, for he prophesies in the name of Illuriel — Ah! They are singing the wine-song, the chant of the nobles. The Queens are singing. How merry they are! — I should like to be a noble and sit and look at the Queens. (*He joins in the song*)

THE VOICE OF A SENTINEL

Guard, turn out. (*The wine-song still continues*)

THE VOICE OF ONE HAVING AUTHORITY

Turn out the guard there! Wake up, you accursed pigs!

[*Still the wine-song. A faint sound as of swords.*

A VOICE CRYING

To the armory! To the armory! Reinforce! The Slaves have come to the armory. Ah! mercy! (*For awhile there is silence*)

KING ARGIMENES (*in the doorway*)

Go you to the slave-fields. Say that the palace-guard is dead and that we have taken the armory. Ten of you, hold the armory till our men come from the slave-fields. (*He comes into the hall with his slaves armed with swords*) Throw down Illuriel.

THE IDOL-GUARD

You must take my life before you touch my god.

A SLAVE

We only want your pike.

[*All attack him; they seize his sword and bind his hands behind him. They all pull down Illuriel, the dark-green idol, who breaks into seven pieces.*

KING ARGIMENES

Illuriel is fallen and broken asunder.

ZARB (*with some awe*)

Immortal Illuriel is dead at last.

KING ARGIMENES

My god was broken into three pieces, but Illuriel is broken into seven. The fortunes of Darniak will prevail over mine no longer. (*A slave breaks off a golden arm from the throne*) Come, we will arm all the slaves. (*Exeunt*)

KING DARNIAK (*enters with Retinue*)

My throne is broken. Illuriel is turned against me.

AN ATTENDANT

Illuriel is fallen.

ALL (*with King Darniak*)

Illuriel is fallen, is fallen. (*Some drop their spears*)

KING DARNIAK (*to the Idol-Guard*)

What envious god or sacrilegious man has dared to do this thing?

THE IDOL-GUARD

Illuriel is fallen.

KING DARNIAK

Have men been here?

THE IDOL-GUARD

Is fallen.

KING DARNIAK

What way did they go?

THE IDOL-GUARD

Illuriel is fallen.

KING DARNIAK

They shall be tortured here before Illuriel, and their eyes shall be hung on a thread about his neck, so that Illuriel shall see it, and on their bones we will set him up again. Come!

[*Those that have dropped their spears pick them up, but trail them along behind them on the ground. All follow dejectedly.*

VOICES OF LAMENTATION (*growing fainter and fainter off*) Illuriel is fallen, Illuriel is fallen. Illuriel, Illuriel, Illuriel. Is fallen. Is fallen. (*The song of the low-born ceases suddenly. Then voices of the slaves in the slave-fields chanting very loudly*) Illuriel is fallen, is fallen, is fallen. Illuriel is fallen and broken asunder. Illuriel is fallen, fallen, fallen.

[*Clamor of fighting is heard, the clash of swords, and voices, and now and then the name of Illuriel.*

THE IDOL-GUARD (*kneeling over a fragment of Illuriel*) Illuriel is broken. They have overthrown Illuriel. They have done great harm to the courses of the stars. The moon will be turned to blackness or fall and forsake the nights. The sun will rise no more.

They do not know how they have wrecked the world.
[*Reënter King Argimenes and his men.*

KING ARGIMENES (*in the doorway*)

Go you to the land of Ithara and tell them that I
am free. And do you go to the army on the frontier. Offer them death, or the right arm of the
throne to be melted and divided amongst them all.
Let them choose. (*The armed slaves go to the
throne and stand on each side of it, loquitur*) Majesty, ascend your throne. (*King Argimenes, standing with his face toward the audience, lifts the sword
slowly, lying on both his hands, a little above his
head, then looking up at it, loquitur*) Praise to the
unknown warrior and to all gods that bless him.
(*He ascends the throne. Zarb prostrates himself
at the foot of it and remains prostrated for the rest
of the Act, muttering at intervals " Majesty." An
armed slave enters dragging the King's Overseer.
King Argimenes sternly watches him. He is dragged
before the Throne. He still has the roll of parchment in his hand. For some moments King Argimenes does not speak. Then pointing at the parchment*) What have you there?

THE KING'S OVERSEER (*kneeling*)

It is a plan of the great garden, Majesty. It was
to have been a wonder to the world. (*Unfolds it*)

KING ARGIMENES (*grimly*)

Show me the place that I digged for three years.
(*The King's Overseer shows it with trembling hands;
the parchment shakes visibly*) Let there be built
there a temple to an Unknown Warrior. And let
this sword be laid on its altar evermore, that the
ghost of that Warrior wandering by night (if men

do walk by night from across the grave) may see his sword again. And let slaves be allowed to pray there and those that are oppressed; nevertheless the noble and the mighty shall not fail to repair there too, that the Unknown Warrior shall not lack due reverence.

[*Enter, running, a Man of the household of King Darniak. He starts and stares aghast on seeing King Argimenes.*

KING ARGIMENES

Who are you?

MAN

I am the servant of the King's dog.

KING ARGIMENES

Why do you come here?

MAN

The King's dog is dead.

KING ARGIMENES AND HIS MEN (*savagely and hungrily*) Bones!

KING ARGIMENES (*remembering suddenly what has happened and where he is*) Let him be buried with the late King.

ZARB (*in a voice of protest*)

Majesty!

CURTAIN

THE GLITTERING GATE

PERSONS

JIM, *lately a burglar* ⎤
BILL, " " " ⎦ *Both dead*

Scene: *A Lonely Place.*
Time: *The present.*

THE GLITTERING GATE

The Lonely Place is strewn with large black rocks and uncorked beer-bottles, the latter in great profusion. At back is a wall of granite built of great slabs, and in it the Gate of Heaven. The door is of gold.

Below the Lonely Place is an abyss hung with stars.

The rising curtain reveals Jim wearily uncorking a beer-bottle. Then he tilts it slowly and with infinite care. It proves to be empty. Faint and unpleasant laughter is heard off. This action and the accompanying far laughter are repeated continually throughout the play. Corked bottles are discovered lying behind rocks, and more descend constantly through the air, within reach of Jim. All prove to be empty.

Jim uncorks a few bottles.

JIM (*weighing one carefully*)
That's a full one. (*It is empty, like all*)
[*Singing is heard off left.*
BILL (*enters from left with a bullet-hole over his eye, singing*) Rule Britannia, Britannia rule the waves. (*Breaking off his song*) Why, 'ullo. 'Ere's a bottle of beer. (*Finds it empty; looking off and downward*) I'm getting a bit tired of those blooming great stars down there and this rocky ledge. I've been walking along under this wall ever since. Why, it must be twenty-four hours since that householder shot me. And he need n't have done it,

either, *I* was n't going to hurt the bloke. I only wanted a bit of his silver stuff. It felt funny, that did. Hullo, a gate. Why, that 's the Gate of Heaven. Well, well. So that 's all right. (*Looks up and up for some time*) No. I can't climb *that* wall. Why, it 's got no top to it. Up and up it goes. (*Knocks at the door and waits*)

JIM

That is n't for the likes of us.

BILL

Why, hullo, there 's another bloke. Why, somebody 's been hanging him. Why, if it is n't old Jim! Jim!

JIM (*wearily*)

Hullo.

BILL

Why, Jim! 'Ow long 'ave you been 'ere?

JIM

I *am* 'ere always.

BILL

Why, Jim, don't you remember me? Why, you taught Bill to pick locks years and years ago when he was a little boy, and had never learnt a trade and had n't a penny in the world, and never would have had but for you, Jim. (*Jim stares vaguely*) I never forgot *you*, Jim. I broke into scores of houses. And then I took on big houses. Out in the country, you know, real big ones. I got rich, Jim, and respected by all who knew me. I was a citizen, Jim, one who dwelt in our midst. And of an evening, sitting over the fire, I used to say, "I am as clever as Jim." But I was n't, Jim. I could n't climb like you. And I could n't walk like you on a creaky stair, when everything's quite still and there's a dog in the house and little rattly things left lying about, and a door that whines if you touch it, and someone ill upstairs that you did n't know of, who has nothing to do but to listen for *you* 'cause she can't get to sleep. Don't you remember little Bill?

JIM

That would be somewhere else.

BILL

Yes, Jim, yes. Down on Earth.

JIM

But there is n't anywhere else.

BILL

I never forgot *you*, Jim. I'd be pattering away with my tongue, in Church, like all the rest, but all the time I'd be thinking of you in that little room at Putney and the man searching every corner of it for you with a revolver in one hand and a candle in the other, and you almost going round with him.

JIM

What is Putney?

BILL

Oh, Jim, can't you remember? Can't you remember the day you taught me a livelihood? I was n't more than twelve, and it was spring, and all the may was in blossom outside the town. And we cleared out No. 25 in the new street. And next day we saw the man's fat, silly face. It was thirty years ago.

JIM

What are years?

BILL

Oh, *Jim!*

JIM

You see there is n't any hope here. And when there is n't any hope there is n't any future. And when there is n't any future there is n't any past. It 's just the present here. I tell you we 're stuck. There are n't no years here. Nor no nothing.

BILL

Cheer up, Jim. You 're thinking of a quotation, " Abandon hope, all ye that enter here." I used to learn quotations; they are awfully genteel. A fellow called Shakespeare used to make them. But there is n't any sense in them. What 's the use of saying *ye* when you mean *you?* Don't be thinking of quotations, Jim.

JIM

I tell you there is no hope here.

BILL

Cheer up, Jim. There 's plenty of hope there, is n't there? (*Points to the Gate of Heaven*)

JIM

Yes, and that 's why they keep it locked up so. They won't let us have any. No. I begin to remember Earth again now since you 've been speaking. It was just the same there. The more they 'd got the more they wanted to keep *you* from having a bit.

BILL

You 'll cheer up a bit when I tell you what I 've got. I say, Jim, have you got some beer? Why, so you have. Why, *you* ought to cheer up, Jim.

JIM

All the beer you 're ever likely to see again. They 're empty.

BILL (*half rising from the rock on which he has seated himself, and pointing his finger at Jim as he rises; very cheerfully*) Why, you 're the chap that said there was no hope here, and you 're hoping to find beer in every bottle you open.

JIM

Yes; I *hope* to see a drop of beer in one some day, but I *know* I won't. Their trick *might* not work just once.

BILL

How many have you tried, Jim?

JIM

Oh, I don't know. I 've always been at it, working as fast as I can, ever since — ever since — (*Feels his neck meditatively and up toward his ear*) Why, ever since, Bill.

BILL

Why don't you stop it?

JIM

I 'm too thirsty, Bill.

BILL

What do you think *I 've* got, Jim?

JIM

I don't know. Nothing 's any use.

BILL (*as yet another bottle is shown to be empty*) Who 's that laughing, Jim?

JIM (*astonished at such a question, loudly and emphatically*) Who 's that laughing?

BILL (*looks a little disconcerted at having apparently asked a silly question*) Is it a pal?

JIM

A pal! — (*laughs*) (*The laugh off joins in loudly and for long*)

BILL

Well, I don't know. But, Jim, what do you think I 've got?

JIM

It is n't any good to you whatever it is. Not even if it is a ten-pound note.

BILL

It 's better than a ten-pound note, Jim. Jim, try and remember, Jim. Don't you remember the way we used to go for those iron safes? Do you remember anything, Jim?

JIM

Yes, I am beginning to remember now. There used to be sunsets. And then there were great yellow lights. And one went in behind them through a swinging door.

BILL

Yes, yes, Jim. That was the Blue Bear down at Wimbledon.

JIM

Yes, and the room was all full of golden light. And there was beer with light in it, and some would be spilt on the counter and there was light in that too. And there was a girl standing there with yellow hair. She 'd be the other side of that door now, with lamplight in her hair among the angels, and the old smile on her lips if one of them chaffed her, and her pretty teeth a-shining. She would be very near the throne; there was never any harm in Jane.

BILL

No, there was never any 'arm in Jane, Jim.

JIM

Oh, I don't want to see the angels, Bill. But if I

could see Jane again (*points in direction of laugh*)
he might laugh as much as he cared to whenever I
wanted to cry. You can't cry here, you know, Bill.

BILL

You shall see her again, Jim.
[*Jim takes no interest in this remark; he lowers his
eyes and goes on with his work.*

BILL

Jim, you shall see her again. You want to get into
Heaven, don't you?

JIM (*not raising his eyes*)
Want!

BILL

Jim. Do you know what I 've got, Jim?
[*Jim makes no answer, goes on wearily with his
work.*

BILL

You remember those iron safes, Jim, how we used
to knock them open like walnuts with " Old Nut-
cracker "?

JIM (*at work, wearily*)
Empty again.

BILL

Well, I 've got Old Nut-cracker. I had him in my
hand at the time, and they let me keep him. They
thought it would be a nice proof against me.

JIM

Nothing is any good here.

BILL

I 'll get in to Heaven, Jim. And you shall come
with me because you taught me a livelihood. I
could n't be happy there, like those angels, if I

knew of anyone being outside. I'm not like that.
[*Jim goes on with his work.*

BILL

Jim, Jim. You'll see Jane there.

JIM

You'll never get through those gates, Bill. You'll
never do it.

BILL

They're only gold, Jim. Gold's soft like lead. Old
Nut-cracker would do it if they were steel.

JIM

You'll never do it, Bill.
[*Bill puts a rock against the gates, stands on it to
reach the lock and gets to work on the lock. A good
instrument to use is an egg-whipper. Jim goes on
wearily with his work. As Bill works away, frag-
ments and golden screws begin to fall on the floor.*

BILL

Jim! Old Nut-cracker thinks nothing of it. It's
just like cheese to old Nut-cracker.

JIM

They won't let you do it, Bill.

BILL

They don't know what I've got. I'm getting
through it like cheese, Jim.

JIM

Suppose it's a mile thick. Suppose it's a million
miles thick. Suppose it's a hundred million miles
thick.

BILL

Can't be, Jim. These doors are meant to open
outward. They couldn't do that if they were more

than four inches at the most, not for an Archbishop. They 'd stick.

JIM

You remember that great safe we broke open once, what had coal in it.

BILL

This is n't a safe, Jim, this is Heaven. There 'll be the old saints with their halos shining and flicker-ing, like windows o' wintry nights. (*Creak, creak, creak*) And angels thick as swallows along a cot-tage roof the day before they go. (*Creak, creak, creak*) And orchards full of apples as far as you can see, and the rivers of Tigris and Euphrates, so the Bible says; and a city of gold, for those that care for cities, all full of precious stones; but I 'm a bit tired of cities and precious stones. (*Creak, creak, creak*) I 'll go out into the fields where the orchards are, by the Tigris and the Euphrates. I should n't be surprised if my old mother was there. She never cared much for the way I earned my livelihood (*creak, creak*), but she was a good mother to me. I don't know if they want a good mother in there who would be kind to the angels and sit and smile at them when they sang and soothe them if they were cross. If they let all the good ones in she 'll be there all right. (*Suddenly*) Jim! They won't have brought me up against her, will they? That 's not fair evidence, Jim.

JIM

It would be just like them to. Very like them.

BILL

If there 's a glass of beer to be got in Heaven, or a dish of tripe and onions, or a pipe of 'bacca she 'll

have them for me when I come to her. She used
to know my ways wonderful; and what I liked.
And she used to know when to expect me almost
anywhere. I used to climb in through the window
at any hour and she always knew it was me. (*Creak,
creak*) She 'll know it 's me at the door now, Jim.
(*Creak, creak*) It will be all a blaze of light, and
I 'll hardly know it 's her till I get used to it. . . .
But I 'll know her among a million angels. There
were n't none like her on Earth and there won't be
none like her in Heaven. . . . Jim! I 'm through,
Jim! One more turn, and old Nut-cracker 's done
it! It 's giving! It 's giving! I know the feel of
it. *Jim!*

[*At last there is a noise of falling bolts; the gates
'swing out an inch and are stopped by the rock.*

BILL

Jim! Jim! I 've opened it, Jim. I 've opened the
Gate of Heaven! Come and help me.

JIM (*looks up for a moment with open mouth. Then
he mournfully shakes his head and goes on drawing
a cork*) Another one empty.

BILL (*looks down once into the abyss that lies below
the Lonely Place*) Stars. Blooming great stars.
[*Then he moves away the rock on which he stood.
The gates move slowly. Jim leaps up and runs to
help; they each take a gate and move backward
with their faces against it.*

BILL

Hullo, mother! You there? Hullo! You there?
It 's Bill, mother.
[*The gates swing heavily open, revealing empty night
and stars.*

BILL (*staggering and gazing into the revealed Nothing, in which far stars go wandering*) Stars. Blooming great stars. There *ain't* no Heaven, Jim.

[*Ever since the revelation a cruel and violent laugh has arisen off. It increases in volume and grows louder and louder.*

JIM

That's like them. That's very like them. Yes, they'd do that!

The curtain falls and the laughter still howls on.

THE LOST SILK HAT

PERSONS

THE CALLER
THE LABORER
THE CLERK
THE POET
THE POLICEMAN

Scene: A fashionable London street.

THE LOST SILK HAT

The Caller stands on a doorstep, "faultlessly dressed," but without a hat. At first he shows despair, then a new thought engrosses him.

Enter the Laborer.

THE CALLER

Excuse me a moment. Excuse me — but — I 'd be greatly obliged to you if — if you could see your way — in fact, you can be of great service to me if —

THE LABORER

Glad to do what I can, sir.

CALLER

Well, all I really want you to do is just to ring that bell and go up and say — er — say that you 've come to see to the drains, or anything like that, you know, and get hold of my hat for me.

LABORER

Get hold of your 'at!

CALLER

Yes. You see, I left my hat behind most unfortunately. It 's in the drawing-room (*points to window*), that room there, half under the long sofa, the far end from the door. And if you could possibly go and get it, why I 'd be (*The Laborer's expression changes*) — Why, what 's the matter?

LABORER (*firmly*)

I don't like this job.

CALLER

Don't like this job! But my dear fellow, don't be silly, what possible harm — ?

LABORER

Ah-h. That's what I don't know.

CALLER

But what harm can there possibly be in so simple a request? What harm does there seem to be?

LABORER

Oh, it seems all right.

CALLER

Well, then.

LABORER

All these crack jobs do seem all right.

CALLER

But I'm not asking you to rob the house.

LABORER

Don't seem as if you are, certainly, but I don't like the looks of it; what if there's things what I can't 'elp taking when I gets inside?

CALLER

I only want my hat. — Here, I say, please don't go away — here's a sovereign, it will only take you a minute.

LABORER

What I want to know —

CALLER

Yes?

LABORER

— Is what's *in* that hat?

CALLER

What's *in* the hat?

LABORER

Yes; that's what I want to know.

CALLER

What's *in* the hat?

LABORER

Yes, you are n't going to give me a sovereign — ?

CALLER

I 'll give you two sovereigns.

LABORER

You are n't going to give me a sovereign, and rise it to two sovereigns, for an *empty* hat?

CALLER

But I must have my hat. I can't be seen in the streets like this. There 's nothing *in* the hat. What do you think 's in the hat?

LABORER

Ah, I 'm not clever enough to say that, but it looks as if the papers was in that hat.

CALLER

The papers?

LABORER

Yes, papers proving, if you can get them, that you 're the heir to that big house, and some poor innocent will be defrauded.

CALLER

Look here, the hat 's absolutely empty. I *must* have my hat. If there 's anything in it you shall have it yourself as well as the two pounds, only get me my hat.

LABORER

Well, that seems all right.

CALLER

That 's right, then you 'll run up and get it?

LABORER

Seems all right to me and seems all right to you.
But it's the police what you and I have got to
think of.   Will it seem all right to them?

CALLER

Oh, for heaven's sake —

LABORER

Ah!

CALLER

What a hopeless fool you are.

LABORER

Ah!

CALLER

Look here.

LABORER

Ah, I got you there, mister.

CALLER

Look here, for goodness sake don't go.

LABORER

Ah!   (*Exit*)

[*Enter the Clerk.*

CALLER

Excuse me, sir.   Excuse my asking you, but, as
you see, I am without a hat.   I shall be extraordi-
narily obliged to you if you would be so very good
as to get it for me.   Pretend you have come to wind
the clocks, you know.   I left it in the drawing-
room of this house, half under the long sofa, the
far end.

CLERK

Oh, er — all right, only —

CALLER

Thanks so much, I am immensely indebted to you.

Just say you 've come to wind the clocks, you know.

CLERK

I — er — don't think I 'm very good at winding clocks, you know.

CALLER

Oh, that 's all right, just stand in front of the clock and fool about with it. That 's all they ever do. I must warn you there 's a lady in the room.

CLERK

Oh!

CALLER

But that 's all right, you know. Just walk past up to the clock.

CLERK

But I think, if you don't mind, as there 's someone there —

CALLER

Oh, but she 's quite young and very, very beautiful and —

CLERK

Why don't you get it yourself?

CALLER

That is impossible.

CLERK

Impossible?

CALLER

Yes, I have sprained my ankle.

CLERK

Oh! Is it bad?

CALLER

Yes, very bad indeed.

CLERK

I don't mind trying to carry you up.

CALLER

No, that would be worse. My foot has to be kept on the ground.

CLERK

But how will you get home?

CALLER

I can walk all right on the flat.

CLERK

I'm afraid I have to be going on. It's rather later than I thought.

CALLER

But for goodness sake don't leave me. You can't leave me here like this without a hat.

CLERK

I'm afraid I must, it's later than I thought. (*Exit*)

[*Enter the Poet.*

CALLER

Excuse me, sir. Excuse my stopping you. But I should be immensely obliged to you if you would do me a very great favor. I have unfortunately left my hat behind while calling at this house. It is half under the long sofa, at the far end. If you could possibly be so kind as to pretend you have come to tune the piano and fetch my hat for me I should be enormously grateful to you.

POET

But why cannot you get it for yourself?

CALLER

I cannot.

POET

If you would tell me the reason perhaps I could help you.

CALLER

I cannot. I can never enter that house again.

POET

If you have committed a murder, by all means tell me. I am not sufficiently interested in ethics to wish to have you hanged for it.

CALLER

Do I look like a murderer?

POET

No, of course not. I am only saying that you can safely trust me, for not only does the statute book and its penalties rather tend to bore me, but murder itself has always had a certain fascination for me. I write delicate and fastidious lyrics, yet, strange as it may appear, I read every murder trial, and my sympathies are always with the prisoner.

CALLER

But I tell you I am not a murderer.

POET

Then what have you done?

CALLER

I have quarrelled with a lady in that house and have sworn to join the Bosnians and die in Africa.

POET

But this is beautiful.

CALLER

Unfortunately I forgot my hat.

POET

You go to die for a hopeless love, and in a far country; it was the wont of the troubadours.

CALLER

But you will get my hat for me?

POET

That I will gladly do for you. But we must find an adequate reason for entering the house.

CALLER

You pretend to tune the piano.

POET

That, unfortunately, is impossible. The sound of a piano being unskilfully handled is to me what the continual drop of cold water on the same part of the head is said to be in countries where that interesting torture is practised. There is —

CALLER

But what are we to do?

POET

There is a house where kind friends of mine have given me that security and comfort that are a poet's necessity. But there was a governess there and a piano. It is years and years since I was able even to see the faces of those friends without an inward shudder.

CALLER

Well, we'll have to think of something else.

POET

You are bringing back to these unhappy days the romance of an age of which the ballads tell us that kings sometimes fought in no other armor than their lady's nightshirt.

CALLER

Yes, but you know first of all I must get my *hat*.

POET

But why?

CALLER

I cannot possibly be seen in the streets without a hat.

POET

Why not?

CALLER

It can't be done.

POET

But you confuse externals with essentials.

CALLER

I don't know what you call essentials, but being decently dressed in London seems pretty essential to me.

POET

A hat is not one of the essential things of life.

CALLER

I don't want to appear rude, but my hat is n't quite like yours.

POET

Let us sit down and talk of things that matter, things that will be remembered after a hundred years. (*They sit*) Regarded in this light one sees at once the triviality of hats. But to die, and die beautifully for a hopeless love, that is a thing one could make a lyric about. That is the test of essential things — try and imagine them in a lyric. One could not write a lyric about a hat.

CALLER

I don't care whether you could write a lyric about my hat or whether you could n't. All I know is that I am not going to make myself absolutely ridiculous by walking about in London without a hat. Will you get it for me or will you not?

POET

To take any part in the tuning of a piano is impossible to me.

CALLER

Well, pretend you 've come to look at the radiator. They have one under the window, and I happen to know it leaks.

POET

I suppose it has an artistic decoration on it.

CALLER

Yes, I think so.

POET

Then I decline to look at it or to go near it. I know these decorations in cast iron. I once saw a pot-bellied Egyptian god, named Bēs, and he was *meant* to be ugly, but he was n't as ugly as these decorations that the twentieth century can make with machinery. What has a plumber got to do with art that he should dare to attempt decoration?

CALLER

Then you won't help me.

POET

I won't look at ugly things and I won't listen to ugly noises, but if you can think of any reasonable plan I don't mind helping you.

CALLER

I can think of nothing else. You don't look like a plumber or a clock-winder. I can think of nothing more. I have had a terrible ordeal and I am not in the condition to think calmly.

POET

Then you will have to leave your hat to its altered destiny.

CALLER

Why can't you think of a plan? If you're a poet, thinking's rather in your line.

POET

If I could bring my thoughts to contemplate so absurd a thing as a hat for any length of time no doubt I could think of a plan, but the very triviality of the theme seems to scare them away.

CALLER (*rising*)

Then I must get it myself.

POET

For Heaven's sake, don't do that! Think what it means!

CALLER

I know it will seem absurd, but not so absurd as walking through London without it.

POET

I don't mean that. But you will make it up. You will forgive each other, and you will marry her and have a family of noisy, pimply children like everyone else, and Romance will be dead. No, don't ring that bell. Go and buy a bayonet, or whatever one does buy, and join the Bosnians.

CALLER

I tell you I can't without a hat.

POET

What is a hat! Will you sacrifice for it a beautiful doom? Think of your bones, neglected and forgotten, lying forlornly because of hopeless love on endless golden sands. "Lying forlorn!" as Keats said. What a word! Forlorn in Africa. The careless Bedouins going past by day, at night the lion's roar, the grievous voice of the desert.

CALLER

As a matter of fact, I don't think you 're right in speaking of it as desert. The Bosnians, I believe, are only taking it because it is supposed to be the most fertile land in the world.

POET

What of that? You will not be remembered by geography and statistics, but by golden-mouthed Romance. And that is how Romance sees Africa.

CALLER

Well, I 'm going to get my hat.

POET

Think! Think! If you enter by that door you will never fall among the foremost Bosnians. You will never die in a far-off, lonely land to lie by immense Sahara. And she will never weep for your beautiful doom and call herself cruel in vain.

CALLER

Hark! She is playing the piano. It seems to me that she might be unhappy about it for years. I don't see much good in that.

POET

No. *I* will comfort her.

CALLER

I 'm damned if you do! Look here! I don't mind saying, I 'm damned if you do.

POET

Calm yourself. Calm yourself. I do not mean in that way.

CALLER

Then what on earth do you mean?

POET

I will make songs about your beautiful death, glad

songs and sad songs. They shall be glad because they tell again the noble tradition of the troubadours, and sad because they tell of your sorrowful destiny and of your hopeless love.

I shall make legends also about your lonely bones, telling perhaps how some Arabian men, finding them in the desert by some oasis, memorable in war, wonder who loved them. And then as I read them to her, she weeps perhaps a little, and I read instead of the glory of the soldier, how it overtops our transitory —

CALLER

Look here, I'm not aware that you've ever been introduced to her.

POET

A trifle, a trifle.

CALLER

It seems to me that you're in rather an undue hurry for me to get a Jubu spear in me; but I'm going to get my hat first.

POET

I appeal to you. I appeal to you in the name of beautiful battles, high deeds, and lost causes; in the name of love-tales told to cruel maidens and told in vain. In the name of stricken hearts broken like beautiful harp-strings, I appeal to you.

I appeal in the ancient holy name of Romance: *do not ring that bell.*

[*Caller rings the bell.*

POET (*sits down, abject*)

You will marry. You will sometimes take a ticket with your wife as far as Paris. Perhaps as far as Cannes. Then the family will come; a large sprawling family as far as the eye can see (I speak in hyperbole). You'll earn money and feed it and be like all the rest. No monument will ever be set up to your memory but—

[*Servant answers bell. Caller says something inaudible. Exit through door.*

POET (*rising, lifting hand*)

But let there be graven in brass upon this house: Romance was born again here out of due time and died young. (*He sits down*)

[*Enter Laborer and Clerk with Policeman. The music stops.*

POLICEMAN

Anything wrong here?

POET

Everything's wrong. They're going to kill Romance.

POLICEMAN (*to Laborer*)

This gentleman does n't seem quite right somehow.

LABORER

They're none of them quite right to-day.

[*Music starts again.*

POET

My God! It is a duet.

POLICEMAN

He seems a bit wrong somehow.

LABORER

You should 'a seen the other one.

CURTAIN